Scuff Marks on the Ceiling

Scuff Marks on the Ceiling

Enjoying
(and Surviving)
Your Child's
Early School Years

Denise Turner

WORD BOOKS
PUBLISHER
WACO, TEXAS

A DIVISION OF
WORD, INCORPORATED

SCUFF MARKS ON THE CEILING: ENJOYING (AND SURVIVING) YOUR
CHILD'S EARLY SCHOOL YEARS

Scripture quotations are from the following sources:
    King James Version of the Bible (KJV).
    The New English Bible (NEB), © 1961, 1970 The Delegates of the Oxford
University Press and the Syndics of Cambridge University Press.
    The Revised Standard Version of the Bible (RSV), copyrighted 1946, 1953,
© 1971, 1973 by the Division of Christian Education of the National Council
of Churches of Christ in the U.S.A.
    The Living Bible Paraphrased (TLB), © 1971 by Tyndale House Publishers.
The Good News Bible, the Bible in Today's English Version (TEV). Copyright
© American Bible Society, 1976.

For information on registered trademarks used in this book see page 185.

Library of Congress Cataloging-in-Publication Data

Turner, Denise.
    Scuff marks on the ceiling.

    Bibliography: p.
    1. Parenting—United States.   2. Parenting—Religious
aspects—Christianity.   3. Child rearing—United States.
I. Title.
HQ755.8.T87   1986   649'.1   86-13316
ISBN 0-8499-0513-3

Printed in the United States of America

6 7 8 9 8   BKC   9 8 7 6 5 4 3 2 1

To my own parents,
for whom I gained an enormous amount of respect
the day I changed my first child's first diaper.

Contents

Acknowledgments

My thanks to Vern Adams, for always being ready to help; the Borlands, who taught me all about unconditional love; John and Paula Dick, friends who support me—and who know what it's like to be real parents; Dr. Richard Dietz and staff, who recently helped me bring into the world enough subject matter for a second book on parenting; Ron Gorby, whose blessing upon my home and my heart has sustained me through the years; Dr. Ronald Solar, Dr. Kenton Pate, and staff, for answering a new mother's stupid questions with straight faces; Dr. Kenneth Story, for teaching me what people are all about; Mimi Smith and Raetta Teager, for opening up their family lives to me; Aunt Alice and Uncle Bud, who loved me as a child and still love me anyway; Mom and Dad Turner, for giving birth to the person who shares my life so perfectly; Rosedale Elementary School staff and parents, for giving this parent a panoramic view of the world of children; Floyd Thatcher and the staff of *Word Books,* for career encouragement of the best kind; the First Baptist Church of Middletown, Ohio, my rock and my strength; and all those who love and nurture me in my Christian pilgrimage. Special thanks to my husband, Revis; our daughter, Rebecca Jill; and our new baby, Stephen Robert—the people who share the very core of my life, the people, because of whom, everything else is worth it.

Introduction

This is a book about children—all children, your children. It is a book designed to help you enjoy your children more, a book designed to help you better perform your task of being a Christian mother or father in today's crazy, mixed-up world. It is not a book which will teach you how to be a perfect parent. I couldn't write a book like that anyway, for I have never come anywhere close to being one. In fact, there are many days when I am sure that I don't understand kids at all. And just as many days when I am not sure I even want to. A case in point . . .

I once made the mistake of allowing my daughter, Becky, at age seven, to invite four of her little friends to dinner on the same night. For a while, I thought I was going to get out of the mess without any battle scars. But then one of the kids decided he wasn't going to eat the noodle casserole.

"Jimmy won't eat something unless he can tell for sure what it is by looking at it," Becky explained. "You know, like the noodles sitting in one place and the cheese somewhere else."

I decided to ignore this and turn my attention toward six-year-old Jason. "Do you need your hamburger cut up, dear?" I asked him.

"No, he doesn't," Becky interrupted. "He just mashes his food up like that when he doesn't like it."

"How do you know so much?" I snapped, fully realizing that I was scheduled to speak on developing positive self-images in children the following day. "You sure weren't that smart last week."

By that time, nothing I could have said would have mattered anyway, because little Julie was screaming, "Jason made me stick my hands in my green beans," and another kid, whose name I never can remember (probably for deeply ingrained subconscious

11

reasons) was whining, "I wish I had a can of Sprite so I could shake it up and point it at crybaby Julie." That was when Jason joined in with the real clincher. "Hey, Julie," he smiled, "did you know Mrs. Turner made the coleslaw out of your Cabbage Patch doll?" And total pandemonium broke loose.

And yet, in spite of it all, I must admit that I do find the job of parenting to be a lot of fun. Not every day, of course; but at least a majority of the time. I often wonder if I am alone in my feelings. For, in my seventeen years of working with Christian families as a minister's wife, I haven't seen too many parents having fun with their kids. Mostly, I see them sending out messages like "Mommy said no" or "Daddy's tired."

In this book, I have chosen to concentrate on the early school years, the formative developmental years of ages five through eight—and on the task of raising children to be happy, productive Christians in today's world. I have frequently read that parents actually know very little about their children during their early school years (at least in part because the children have begun to pull away from home and build strong bonds with other children). I have no trouble believing that. It's hard to practice the fine art of in-depth communication with someone who has a Walkman permanently attached to his head.

Each child in the world has been created by God as a unique individual who develops and grows at his own rate. Most of us are well aware of this fact. And yet, I think we can learn a lot by observing how other families handle situations that are similar to our own. It is this kind of learning that I am attempting to encourage and to share in this book.

Of course, I know full well that there are some parents who have already, for all practical purposes, given up on the whole thing. They say they fear it is impossible to raise decent kids in today's society. "There is too much sin in the world," they sigh. "We have simply gone too far." Such parents often end up conceding their rightful places of authority to their children's peer groups—a bunch of people who believe the world was created the same year air conditioning and color TV were invented, a bunch of people who still sleep with their teddy bears.

There is no doubt about it. Every parent in the world has moments when he feels like bailing out, even if it means giving control to those who still sleep with their teddy bears. But we parents have other types of moments, too. Like the day last summer when I was lying on the beach watching my husband, Revis, teach Becky how to build a sand castle. God had provided us with a perfectly blue sky as a backdrop that day, and my little family looked so beautiful against it. . . . It was one of those moments I wanted to eternalize so that I could live it over and over again.

"This is the way life should be," I told myself. But I know it can't always be that way. Just a week later, in fact, Becky caught one of those twenty-four hour viruses, and I spent the night sitting by her bed wondering if I could get her into the *Guinness Book of World Records* for the largest number of trips to the bathroom in one night. Being a parent is like that—from sand castles to diarrhea back to sand castles, all in one fell swoop.

It is both a privilege and a responsibility to be entrusted with God-given life. It can be pretty scary, too. "Will we do everything right?" the new parents ask themselves. (You won't.) "Will our mistakes be fatal ones?" (Not likely.) "Will all of this be worth it in the end?"

I have a friend who raised three happy, healthy, Christian children to adulthood. My friend is not perfect. She wouldn't hang around with me if she were. But she came out okay. "Was it worth all the trouble?" I once asked her; and, with tears in her eyes, she spoke some words that I will never forget. "To see your children born is magnificent," she said, "but to see them reborn is indescribable."

Christian parenting can be both effective and fun. If we keep working at it. If we keep looking for ways to put the joy and purpose into it. This book is designed to reveal some of those ways.

In the following pages you will find information and ideas about children's behavioral styles, emotional development, value systems, and religious education. You will also find suggestions about how you can put more fun into your home life and handle the pressures involved in building a happy marriage and family life in today's world.

Parenting can be more fun than you ever imagined it could be—maybe, the most fun you can have without calories. Sure there are parents in the world who only think in terms of surviving until the last child leaves home, but I firmly believe it doesn't have to be like that. I'm convinced that children are meant to be enjoyed—even in those early school years when they seem to be bouncing off the walls, even when there are scuff marks on the ceiling.

Prologue

A Quick Look at the Very Early Years

Almost from the moment of conception, I found myself forced to sift through the propaganda. "Your life is never going to be the same," my own mother told me, with what I thought was a rather sinister smile. "A lot of parents refer to the hour between 6:00 and 7:00 P.M., not as the dinner hour, but as the arsenic hour," insisted a friend. "Here's How to Know if You're Ready to Have a Baby," the title of the magazine article assured me in big bold type; but I was already eight months pregnant at the time. I needed an article entitled "Ready or Not, Here Comes Baby."

The strange thing about all of this is that most of what you hear is true, at least to some extent. Anne Follis, in her book *I'm Not a Women's Libber, But . . . ,* contends that having small children around is a lot like being nibbled to death by ducks. And, in describing the first few years of parenthood, I suspect that her words are as accurate as any could possibly be.

When our first child was born, my husband and I felt like life on this planet, as we had known it, had suddenly been turned inside out. We were robbed of both privacy and sleep. Sit-down dinners were tossed aside in favor of the stand-up variety. There was no opportunity for sex. And we spent most of our free time talking about diaper rash and running into the nursery to see if our daughter was still breathing.

Today, as I look back on it, I can see that most of my struggles

15

during those weeks were compounded by my totally unrealistic expectations about parenting. If you are just starting out as a parent, try to keep this in mind: the more unrealistic your expectations, the harder the struggle. I myself had expected parenthood to be something more akin to eighteen years of bliss than to eighteen years of hard labor. I should have expected something in between. I think it all started when, as a young bride, I clipped out a magazine article about a beautiful blonde woman planning a big holiday party with her obviously super-rich husband. It's been sixteen years now, and I still have the article.

There are lots of pictures of the woman concocting elegant desserts and "popping" them into the freezer weeks ahead, and of the table, decorated in elaborate colors because the couples' china is all white (purposely selected through the years because it "looks great with any color scheme"). The husband, between important business meetings, helps with the invitations; and the wife remains the immaculate vision of serenity and organization, carefully checking each head of cauliflower and planning her party wardrobe with even greater care.

"This is family life," I convinced myself. "Happily ever after." It wasn't until I gave birth to my first child that it dawned on me. Those people didn't have any children.

Having a baby forces you not so much to toss away the dreams, but to infuse them with real life. Being a new parent is not combing shops for the perfect shade of white china. It's more like learning how to cope with what one writer lovingly termed "battle fatigue." You do the same jobs over and over so many times that you begin to see mirages of hired help all around your house. You call the pediatrician ten or twelve times a night, until he finally puts you on hold and leaves you there. And you hear yourself reciting prayers like, "Just help me make it through the day, Lord," or "Thank you so much that it wasn't triplets."

What you are really doing is opening up your world to include a new person in it. You are adding one more intense relationship into the mix. You are launching yourself into the future, and you are going into culture shock at the sudden realization that there are at least two generations now living under the same roof—yours! Last week I heard a report on the radio stating that today's babies will grow up to a twenty-hour work week, stay in the work force until they are seventy-five years old, and go back to school every six years for career retraining. Who knows what else will have happened to our world, good or bad, by the time we are ready to send our children out into it?

And yet, God wanted you to be the parent of that child. No doubt about it. He believed you could do it. From the very moment of birth, that baby began to learn about love and trust from the simple experience of being held and fed by you, all initiated and planned by God, who Himself chose to come to this world in the form of a tiny baby—innocent, precious, fresh from heaven.

Sure, it takes a while for a baby to start giving much back. In the beginning, about all you can hope for is one hour of not having to drop anything into the diaper pail, or one meal without a deposit of soured milk on your clean shirt. But, even at that, there is something to be said for the feel of a baby's soft cheek pressed against yours. And besides, the mess won't last forever. Not in the same form, anyway.

It isn't all that long before a baby starts developing communication skills. In fact, by the time a couple of years have passed, a child has a vocabulary of about 300 words. The only problem is that 290 of them are variations of the word *no*.. A child also quickly learns how to say "Me want" and "Gimmee," and parents have to learn how to differentiate between a necessity, a desire, and an "if you don't give it to me, I'll someday get back at you by growing up, making a million dollars, and telling you I think it would build your character to live on Social Security."

In no time at all your baby makes it to the early school years, the years when you feel certain there must be scuff marks even on the ceiling. And you move into a new stage of parenting, a stage in which you sometimes feel almost as inept as your kids already think you are. I once heard a joke about someone being too dumb to know how to make Kool-Aid because he couldn't figure out how to get two quarts of water into the little envelope. That just about says it, I guess. You have barely learned how to treat cradle cap, and it's already time to start worrying about making the Kool-Aid—and everything else that goes along with it.

1

Ready, Set, Go
Beginning School or Kindergarten

"My son, do not forget my teaching, but guard my commands in your heart."

—Proverbs 3:1, NEB

A school teacher once told me about a first-grade boy who was late for school. Huffing and puffing, the child rushed up to the teacher's desk and held out a crumpled note from his mother. "Please excuse Timmy for being," the note read. "It's his father's fault."

That particular mother probably didn't mean to omit the word *late* from her note, but anyone who has ever been the mother of a grade-school child can certainly identify with the unintended sentiment it expressed. Elementary school is the beginning of a whole new world, both for the child and for the parent.

The world of the grade-school child is kind of like a kaleidoscope of soccer and ballet and scouting and church choir and, somewhere behind the scenes, an exhausted set of parents with an empty gas tank. Your school-age child is moving out into the world; he is making new friends; he is growing up (sort of). At times his reasoning ability will amaze you. Take for example the logic my friend's seven-year-old son used when he informed her one afternoon, "Since I have to chew sugarless gum, you can just buy me sugared gum, and I'll chew the sugar out so it will be sugarless." The following day, this budding young genius missed every word on his second-grade spelling test (including his own name).

Sure, there may be days when the grade-school child will answer the telephone with the words, "Smith residence, Cindy speaking." But there will probably be just as many days when she will answer by singing (to the tune of "Happy Birthday"), "Hello now to you. You live in a zoo. You look like a monkey. You smell like one too."

The Countdown to School Days

Most children are ready for school when the time comes, but parents are sometimes another story. Take my experience, for example. By the time Becky started school, I had been told, many times, that giving birth to a child changes a woman's life; but I had never been told how many day-to-day changes the school years would bring. I had never been told how much my own schedule would begin to revolve around my child.

First came the realization that I would have to listen to the local radio station (which plays only bluegrass music) on bad weather days in order to find out about school delays and early dismissals. (I now know enough about honky-tonk women and jilted cowboys to make it on the Grand Ole Opry myself.)

Next came the school booster shots and a visit to the pediatrician's office jammed full of children who would be limping for days just to show off their new status symbols. But this wasn't, by any means, the most painful part for me. True pain was reserved for the day when the bills for school fees were doled out.

I soon found out I would be paying an initial twenty-five dollars to cover my daughter's school supplies. Then I would have to pay for her school lunches and several "extras" and would even be expected to furnish punch and cups for class refreshment breaks. "What in the world are our taxes paying for?" I asked Revis in frustration one night.

"You're going to have 6½ hours every day when no one is going to be asking you to play hide-and-seek," he replied. Suddenly, twenty-five dollars seemed like a real bargain.

Into the Cold, Cruel World

"Do you have to wait until you go to school to become a dropout?" Becky asked with great seriousness the day before she entered kindergarten.

"I think you have to drop into something before you can drop out of it," I answered, and I was reminded of the time my friend Jan told me that her child was terrified at the prospect of beginning first grade.

"Bobby packed five cookies, an apple, and two pairs of jeans (thinking it would be enough to last a year), and he ran away from home," Jan explained. Of course, Bobby got to the end of his driveway that day and decided to return home because he had to go to the bathroom.

Starting school can be a pretty scary experience for any child, perhaps especially for those who have spent little or no time in preschool or day care. But separation from home and hearth is a fact of life in our world, and it is a fact of life that each of us must learn to handle, over and over again.

The first day Becky left home on a school bus, I found myself thinking of my first solo business trip. I had wanted to go home to the bathroom, too. But home was eight hundred miles away for me.

Still, a little reassurance and a generous dose of empathy can go a long way toward easing the pain. "It's okay to be afraid of going to school," I told my daughter. "I sometimes feel afraid when I try new things, too."

Becky came home that day bubbling with stories about the art teacher who looks just like Aunt Alice—and the little girl who brought her Barbie doll to "Show and Tell" and made all the boys close their eyes whenever she changed Barbie's clothes. Clearly, my child had been initiated into her new life in grand style.

Of course, teaching a child how to deal with his separation anxieties still solves only half a problem. I discovered that particular fact the hard way, shortly after my daughter entered kindergarten, when I began experiencing a little separation anxiety of my own.

Suddenly, for the first time, my child had a life without me.

She would come home talking about people I didn't know and activities I hadn't shared. I tried to get some encouragement from my next-door neighbor during these days, but she told me she still cries whenever her children walk out the door—and they're in junior high now! And so, I was afraid. I was certain that Becky would never be my baby girl again.

For a while, Becky seemed to be doing everything she could to increase my fears. One morning right before she left to catch the school bus, she glanced back at her dad and said, "Do you think I'm sexy enough to attract boys, Daddy?"

Her father was speechless, of course. He stared into space for a long time after she left and mumbled, "I think I was just asked the question that all fathers dread most."

When I went to Becky's school to sign her kindergarten emergency medical forms, I became even more sure that five is the age when you lose them. . . . "I see here that I have only two choices," I said to the school nurse, trying to inject a little humor into a potentially tear-jerking situation. "I can either agree to allow my injured child to receive medical treatment without my consent if you can't reach me, or I can let her die." The nurse didn't smile. She had evidently spent too many years of her life talking about head lice to be able to enjoy a good laugh.

Yes, I had lost my baby. I was certain of it—until the next day, that is, when my "big girl" picked me a Dixie Cup full of dandelions and asked if she could climb up into my lap and rock. "Thank you, Lord," I murmured, knowing, beyond a shadow of a doubt, that my job was far from done.

After that, I concentrated on doing everything I could to prepare my child for her life outside the home, especially since everyone kept telling me how important this is. So, I talked to my child about taking good care of herself; and I enrolled her in a local police-sponsored Safety Town, where she learned all about getting on and off the Big Yellow Fellow (school bus) and never running between Sleeping Lions (two parked cars).

Often, when I arrived at Safety Town to pick up my child, she was driving her little car on the left side of the road—or trying to convince her teacher that carrying a glass of milk on a nighttime walk is just as good as wearing a white shirt. But she did seem to be learning a lot from all this. One Sunday, in fact, she even refused to speak to the guest minister at church because she insisted he was a stranger.

We played quite a few "what if" games at our house during this time. "What if someone offered you a ride in a car?" I would ask. Or, "What if you walked home from Leah's house and Mommy was not there?" I figured we had played these games long enough when I got to, "What if that big dog down the street starts foaming at the mouth and coming toward you late at night?" Becky's answer to that one was, "That dog got run over last month, Mommy. Don't you remember? He ran between two Sleeping Lions. And besides, dogs shouldn't even be out at night because they don't have hands to carry glasses of milk. . . ." From that time on, I grew more and more assured that my child knew enough about getting along in her new world.

"What's the most important thing you've learned about school?" I asked her one day, expecting to be given back some of the good, solid lessons I had taught her.

"When your teacher tells you to go to the bathroom and get your drink," came the quick reply, "she doesn't mean you have to get your drink in the bathroom instead of at the water fountain."

It almost made sense. For, I had just read a newspaper article listing second graders' tips to incoming first graders, one of which was the importance of remembering that the school cafeteria's chocolate ice cream looks just like the vanilla. A bowl of ice cream and a good cold drink—those are the staff of life among grade-school kids. And they even know that the chocolate looks like the vanilla. A tip like that just might take them farther in their world than they think it will.

And so, the child's trek through the school days continues, generally with only minor disasters along the way. However, I must admit that there were times when my husband and I probably should have been a little less attentive. Like the day we hid behind a tree and took elaborate home movies of Becky's first ride on the school bus. I felt pretty silly about that one until a teen-age friend told me about another proud parent, a father who took home movies of his daughter driving to high school on the last day of her senior year.

Obviously, most of us have very similar feelings about our children—we're proud to see them growing up, but we harbor just a twinge of anxiety at the thought of the fate that might await them in the world we are entrusting them to.

Grade Schoolers' Special Needs

You are bound to learn a lot about the needs of school children during your child's first few years of elementary school. One very important need, for instance, comes at the end of a busy, structured school day—the need to unwind and express one's creativity freely and in an environment of acceptance.

"Even though they have been sitting all day, many school-age children choose to spend their after-school hours talking quietly to other children," one day-care director told me. And, of course, there are children who need to jog around a little after school and expend some energy. Children have other needs, too. Sometimes they need to talk about their feelings. Dramatic play and dress up help children express negative emotions. So does dollhouse play or puppet play. In fact, more than a few teachers have assured me that many children, when they have puppets in their hands, will discuss things they wouldn't dare talk about any other time.

Many children enjoy playing school teacher, just to see what it would feel like to be an adult authority figure. Take, for example, the child in our church's after-school, day-care center who was recently acting out her authority role by introducing a new student to the center's "red for right, green for left" color coding system for scissors. "Use the red scissors," the little girl slowly explained, "unless you are green-handed."

This is how our children learn to enjoy their school years. The years of expanded horizons. The years when a child needs so much love and support from his parents as he blazes his new trails.

What's a Room Mother?

I came to terms with the fact that my child was more than ready to take her first step in her journey away from home partly because so many people told me that a positive attitude toward the whole thing is the key to success for both parent and child. They also told me that the next step should center around getting used to a new routine of my own. That is when I started going out to lunch with my husband more, and finding out just how much fun this can be. However, when we were toying with the idea of taking a much longer lunch hour, I got the first call.

"Your daughter says you are so good at crafts, Mrs. Turner," my child's kindergarten teacher purred, "so I thought you might agree to be one of our happy volunteers this year."

"I'm going to kill you, Becky," I mumbled, knowing full well that my child was sitting right beside me when I completed my first and last craft project—a door decoration in which a flock of birds immediately built a nest.

"I'm not sure I'm really qualified for . . . ," I began.

"Just anything with paper plates will be fine for tomorrow," the teacher interrupted in the cheery kind of voice they teach you in elementary education, and she hung up.

I tried crying on friends' shoulders, but most of them were too experienced in the game of parenting to sympathize. "You're lucky," one of them told me. "I got stuck leading the kindergarten nature walk last year, and I ended up with ten kids bawling because they were the only ones who didn't get poison ivy."

Another friend didn't say a word to me. Instead, she took me out and showed me her garage. It was enough. She was the cookie mother for her daughter's Brownie troop.

Eventually, of course, I got used to fulfilling my parental duties at school; and I even learned how to say no once in a while. I also learned that a Christian parent must continually search for that fine balance between knowing when to be there for his children and knowing when to stay away and trust them to God's care.

The dilemma, then, centers around figuring out how involved we should be in our children's learning processes—for it is important to be involved. In fact, even simple activities like listening to our children read and playing learning games with them are thought to be contributing elements in both improved grades and improved behavior at school. Parents need to exhibit healthy attitudes toward their children's teachers and administrators, too. Getting to know those people helps a lot.

Being a grade-school teacher isn't easy. I am sure of it. One child told me that a classmate at school knocked the puzzle rack off the shelf one day and that his teacher had to "stay after school" to put together twelve puzzles from the heap of pieces on the floor. Another child told me his best friend wears the neatest watch to school—the kind that beeps on the hour, every hour. Can you imagine living in that kind of atmosphere each day, and smiling sweetly at the children who (however unintentionally) are trying their best to drive you nuts?

It took only one incident in my own daughter's classroom to persuade me that her teacher deserves my undying support. The teacher had told the children (in a moment of desperation, I suspect) that they could put a marble into a jar every time they were good—and that, when there were one hundred marbles in the jar, they could choose to have any kind of party they wanted. It seemed like a safe deal at the time, I guess. The little terrors sitting in the classroom that day had already convinced their teacher that they couldn't possibly be good until they were at least thirty-five years old. Nevertheless, the teacher soon realized she had left some loopholes in her agreement.

The first loophole was underestimating any child's ability to be good if the payoff appears to be worth it to him. The second loophole was giving an unqualified choice to people whose imaginations are capable of visualizing a world in which Boy George is king. And so, my daughter's teacher ended up planning a "pet party" for her second grade class.

The minute I walked into the school building that day, I knew that Becky's well-behaved, and not particularly exotic, goldfish was definitely not going to be the hit of the party. Dogs were pulling their masters down the halls. Rabbits were hopping out of their boxes. Turtles were hiding in their shells. "And you thought this place was a zoo before," I smiled toward a friend who does some part-time work at the school, but I could tell by her glazed expression that she was already beyond smiling back.

Inside Becky's classroom there were so many four-legged animals that three birds had already keeled over in abject horror. Two little girls, whose parents had evidently failed to tell them that liberated women don't scream and climb up on tables, were sobbing hysterically because a frog named Frankenstein had gotten loose. And several assorted cats were just about to remember they had forgotten to use their litter boxes before they left home. The children were trying to introduce their pets to the class; but, since the noise level in the room had already reached the decibel level of a sold-out rock concert, it was no use.

Luckily, the teacher had required parents to accompany those children who brought in uncaged pets and had instructed the parents not to leave those pets at school during the day. It helped, but not too much. The students were so excited that the only real solution would have been to force the parents to take home any uncaged children, too.

Still, pet day did teach me a lot about empathizing with both teachers and other parents. It also taught me that there are many people in the school system who really like children. And so, I have since come to realize that, although my child kisses me good-bye and disappears from my sight when she leaves for school every morning, she is far from alone while she is there.

They Don't Go to School Alone

There are all kinds of people at school who care about your child. It is important to remember this. Just as it is important to remember that God is never far from your child's side. In fact, there have been many days during my daughter's early school years when I have been able to see, very clearly, how closely God works with little children. Take the day when Becky decided she shouldn't have to share her crayons, for example.

Both her father and I had tried to reason with her, but to no avail. "Please God, teach her to be more loving," was my silent prayer as my child walked out the door that morning. "I don't seem to know how to get through to her this time, so I'll have to leave it up to you."

Becky left for school that day clutching her cherished box of bright new crayons close to her heart, determined never to let anyone touch them. But a little boy at school shared his own new crayons with her that day anyway—and she accidentally broke one of them.

"He just said, 'That's okay,' in a soft little voice, Mommy," Becky later told me in great amazement. "I thought he was going to pull my hair or kick me in the stomach, or at least tell the teacher on me, but he didn't."

How much those words have continued to mean to my child, time and time again. Two simple little words, whispered barely loud enough to hear. "That's okay." The same words my heavenly Father said to me this very morning, and yesterday, and the day before, in almost the same way.

The little boy with the crayons moved away at the end of the school year, before I had even figured out a way to thank him. Maybe he was placed in Becky's class that year for one purpose, or maybe I'm making too much out of it. I don't know. I just know that Becky has never complained about sharing anything with anyone since that experience.

I prayed a lot during my daughter's early school years, but I always knew, deep down inside, that most children, by age five, are ready to tackle anything. So I watched her go out the door to school each day, the hope of the world with a chocolate cupcake smashed in her pocket. And I learned to find peace in the fact that she was moving through the world according to God's plan. She was busy discovering a part of her new life and building the rest of it, but she'd still need help—mine and Revis's and the Lord's.

Parting Tips

As your child gets ready to start school . . .

—Ease him into his routine a little early. Make sure he is getting plenty of sleep and a good, nutritional breakfast. But don't spend all summer dwelling on the subject of school. No matter how young or old he is, he's still entitled to catch his lightning bugs in peace.

—Travel the school route with him for a few days before school starts; and arrange for him to visit the school, meet his teacher, and see his room. (Simply showing him where the bathroom is could well prevent a few needless nightmares.) Make sure he knows his name, address, and phone number too; and send his lunch money in a clearly marked envelope—and never send him off the first day in new clothes and shoes. Let him have the security of a favorite shirt and the comfort of a pair of shoes he's climbed a few trees in.

—Spend some summer time browsing through the public library with him. Introduce him to new kinds of reading materials, and let him reintroduce you to Dr. Seuss. You've spent so many years with a preschooler that the nonsense words in these books will sound almost normal to you.

—Pretend to be extremely domestic for a few days, and sew labels into all his clothes. Don't let his teacher spend the first day of winter the way one grade-school teacher did—shuffling and reshuffling fifteen pairs of size thirteen red boots.

—Keep the communication lines open during these years. Later on you will end up thanking yourself many times over. Be available to your child when he needs you, but don't hang around his school. If you do, you will probably overhear one of the kids talking about how old twenty-one is; and your whole day will be shot.

2

Kid Stuff
Childhood Friendships

"A mirror reflects a man's face, but what he is really like is shown by the kind of friends he chooses."
—Proverbs 27:19, TLB

I think I always expected peer pressure to start affecting my child somewhere around age twelve, but I couldn't have been more wrong.

"Mommy, Jeannie says I have to wear my old blue Strawberry Shortcake shirt to school tomorrow," Becky informed me when she was five.

"And what happens if you don't?" I asked.

"Then a person-eating tiger will come to our house and live with us."

"Person-eating tiger," I smiled to myself. "Well, at least gender consciousness has made it into the kindergarten classroom." But I was still faced with a dilemma of sorts. I could either let my child succumb to her first bout with peer pressure, or I could accept the possibility that a person-eating tiger might come to live with us (or, even worse, Jeannie in a tiger costume might come to live with us).

I decided that my rational arguments about the impossibility of a person-eating tiger coming to live in a house wouldn't sound very logical to someone who still believes in the tooth fairy. So, in order to spare us all a sleepless night, I dug out the blouse. As I laid it out with the next day's school clothes, I think I heard my daughter mumble, "Good, because everybody's going to wear one."

When Peer Pressure Invades the Home

Becky's pleas for conformity had seemed rather cute until the "everybody's doing it" line, but that bothered me a little. Somewhere, in the back of my mind, I think I sensed that these are the very words I might someday have to blame for a teen-age experience with alcohol or a too serious encounter with the opposite sex. "Oh well," I consoled myself, "at least none of the kindergarten girls are wearing bras yet." I did have a little time.

But time does fly, even when you're not always having fun; and I guess it's never too early to think about a little preventive medicine. "Practice staging everyday situations with your children," a minister once told me, "and role play the ways a person can say no to something he doesn't want to do."

"Tell your children there may be other people in the group who won't want to smoke that cigarette either," my Bible study leader advised, "and let them know that their strength could help those other people to say no, too." Lots of parents have also told me they always encouraged their children to feel free, whenever necessary, to use Mom and Dad as scapegoats. Many of those children later told their parents that a fearful-sounding "My dad would absolutely kill me" had gotten them through quite a few tough spots.

A child who has a positive self-image, a child who has a sense of belonging in many different areas of life generally has less trouble with peer pressure. That is why it is so important for children to have good structures to fall back on in church, home, and school life. And yet, nothing can totally negate the power wielded by a youngster's peer group. For, the approval of one's peers is an extremely important factor in the development of a child's social maturity. A wise parent never forgets this, not even for a minute.

"Can I have the secret club meeting at our house this year?" Becky asked me when she was seven. She was using her I'll-

scrub-the-floors-if-I-have-to voice at the time. That was my intro-
duction to the strangest of all middle-childhood phenomenons—
the secret club.

The secret club is probably a spin-off from secret chants, matching wardrobes, and knock-knock jokes (all of which you can remember from your own childhood, but they seemed much funnier
at the time). The secret club meetings that are now held at my
house are held mostly in closets. One day I got up the nerve to
ask why.

"We're looking for the secret door, Mom," Becky said, and I
could tell she thought I was completely out of it for not having
known that. I decided to change the subject.

"Why is Mary sitting in the corner by herself then?"

"Oh, Mom!" my child replied in another silly-Mom-doesn't-
know-anything tone. "She's just the club mascot because she's
the only one who hasn't lost both of her front teeth yet."

And so my daughter sat, with her toothless friends, among a
row of winter coats, for an hour each week. These were not
dumb kids either. These were the children who were winning
the reading and math awards at school.

"Why doesn't my coat fit in the closet anymore?" Revis asked
one day when he got off work early.

"The kids are in there," I answered nonchalantly. "They're looking for the secret door." My spouse accepted my explanation
without question, like any good husband who hasn't read the
sports page yet. A book I was reading at the time assured me
that secret clubs are a normal part of a child's growing up process.
The book even told about one secret club that consisted of five
girls who met every Saturday afternoon under a bridge for the
sole purpose of counting cars and marking down the ones that
needed washing.

When I finished the book, I began to relax a little. Probably
because finding out that there is a possibility, however remote,
that one's child is still normal in spite of it all adds a little zip
to any parent's day.

Parental Involvement—to Pry or Not to Pry

There are lots of reasons not to get involved in our grade-
school children's friendship-building processes, one of which is

the fact that we don't speak their language anymore. Not only is giggling the one accepted form of communication among eight-year-old girls, but the terms used by all grade-school children generally change from week to week. And, no matter what week it is, we are never told what any of the words mean. This is probably for the best.

Another point in favor of noninvolvement is the fact that school-age children usually have variable attitudes toward other children. They often have fights with their best friends and come home insisting that they "never want to see Kelly again because she told the teacher that all the other kids in class got together and ate her pencil." Later in the day, the same child will be begging to ask Kelly over for dinner.

Nevertheless, you must be involved, at least to some extent, in your children's friendships. In fact, a very significant part of the friendship-building process centers around your encouraging your children to invite friends over to the house—which means, among other things, that you must learn to live with all kinds of new frustrations.

The mother of a grade-school child has to be able to carry on telephone conversations with people who haven't really learned to speak in full sentences yet. She also has to be able to smile sweetly at dinner guests who instruct her to make sure the food on their plates doesn't touch or who request separate utensils for each kind of food. (One mother refused such a request, and the child wiped his spoon with his napkin between bites.)

The smart parent soon learns to lock the bathroom door during these years. For these are the years when freckle-faced, dirty-knuckled children you've never seen before in your life can be found wandering through the rooms of your house at the most unexpected moments.

There will also be those times when a parent is drawn into a discussion that he could have lived a perfectly happy life never having heard. For example, Becky ran in from the side yard one day yelling, "Megan said the *B* word; Megan said the *B* word; you better call her mother and tell her."

The "*B* word" turned out to be *but,* and the sentence in which it was used: "Just give me my doll; no ifs, ands, or buts!"

Needless to say, I spent the rest of the afternoon trying to teach a lesson in semantics that no one really cared about. It was one among many days when I would have been just as glad not to be involved in my daughter's friendships.

When Your Child Has Trouble Making Friends

Children who have a happy, solid home life and who are taught to cultivate a good personality and a well-tuned sense of humor are likely to have little trouble making friends. But sometimes they do—and their parents are left wondering how much to interfere.

"Don't take everything too seriously," a wise parent once warned me. "All kids have days when they resort to the grade-school war cry of the ages: 'Everybody hates me!'" My friend did tell me how important it is to talk to your child about his feelings though, and to be there to help him if you think there really is a problem.

Experienced parents usually agree that it is necessary to let the child know that, no matter what she does, not everyone is going to like her; and she is not going to like everyone—and that having someone dislike you doesn't have to keep you from liking yourself. "Most people in the world feel they are lucky if they have only a few good friends," I once told Becky. She was trying to make friends with an ant at the time, by using a crumb of bread to lead him out of the house to freedom so she wouldn't have to smash him.

"She understands what I am telling her," I comforted myself, knowing full well that if I didn't say things like that to myself once in a while, I could end up with a very deflated ego merely from thinking about the great volumes of parental wisdom I so often dispense on deaf ears.

A parent can help enhance his child's friendship-building process in many ways. You can talk to the child's teacher, for instance, and bounce around some ideas to use in planning a few classroom activities designed to improve the friend situation. Or you can encourage the child to invite a friend along on a family picnic; this will help him learn how to better relate to other children, one on one. (After all, two collections of frogs are no worse than one.)

"When a child is having trouble making friends," a school teacher explained, "I usually provide him with something of interest that will draw other children to him." This is much like the picnic idea. Another variation is to choose a day when something interesting is going on at home and let the child invite other children over.

I have one friend who had so much success with this sort of thing that she ended up with fifteen children watching cartoons at her house one Saturday morning, simply because she was "crazy enough" to allow them to make homemade cookies afterwards. (She later told me, "When they decided to nickname me Keebler Elf, I started limiting the number of children to two friends per child per Saturday.") Another mother told me that the sight of a dad out playing ball with his kids is so unusual on her street that anyone who tries this is bound to wind up with several reserve teams plopped on his front lawn—for life if he isn't careful.

One father I know attracts a driveway full of little children to his house every afternoon just because his basketball hoop is low enough for little kids to reach and big kids to "slam dunk." Of course, the day he asked to join in the game, he found out that dads are not always chosen first in the draft merely because they are bigger. Thus, after a ten-minute elimination which was designed to determine the captains, but was halted when no one could make a foul shot, Dad found himself standing with two kindergarten boys, among the last three to be chosen for a team. Everyone had fun though. Even Dad. And the kids kept coming back.

When Your Child Conforms Too Often

Those of us who are "lucky" enough to be the parents of extremely bullheaded children are frequently told that we should take solace in the fact that those are the kind who generally turn out better able to withstand peer pressure in later years. Still, there are some people whose children aren't bullheaded (and they're probably very glad about that), and there are others of us who feel we may never make it to our children's later years.

No matter how many times a parent reminds his children that they are unique individuals, he can't get away from the fact that children need to be like their peers to some extent. There is simply no way around that. True, we may cringe at the sight of our seven-year-olds filing onto the school bus in "uniforms" that were concocted by someone who doesn't even have his permanent teeth yet; but most parents agree that we should save our "absolutely no" edicts for something a little more important than purple knee socks.

Thus, parents may have to let their child choose a birthday gift that appears to have been created by a toy designer who cheated his way through Tiddlywinks 101, or they may have to let the child watch a TV show that he himself could have written at age three—all to help the child get the need to conform out of his system. "If this sounds too lenient," one parent remarked, "think about how you'd feel if you had to go to Little League practice and tell your pals you thought 'Shirt Tales' were something that hung out of pants—and all because your dad makes you watch the 'MacNeil/Lehrer NewsHour' instead of the kiddie shows on TV."

The idea, then, is to make sure we have rules that are both consistent and reasonable—and to have good enough memories to recall how many things we ourselves once felt we would just die if we didn't get.

When Your Child Makes Friends of the Questionable Variety

"From time to time, Johnny used to bring home a friend I didn't like," one mother told me, "but I never said much. I figured he probably didn't like all of my friends either. In fact, I'm not sure *I* really like all of my friends."

God created all human beings of equal worth, and all of us want to get that concept across to our children. But that doesn't make it any easier to sit at the dinner table and look at yet another little person who insists on telling you what your scalloped potatoes "really look like."

Some people suggest that children who regularly choose "losers" as friends might be trying to overcompensate for something they are lacking. Thus, a practical joker who delights in telling off-color stories might be chosen as a friend by a child who is painfully shy. And, it would follow that the concerned parent might be able to make this kind of friend seem less appealing if he could help his child develop a more outgoing personality.

Beyond that, most parents feel that the best advice is to know where your children are, even when it isn't yet 11:00 P.M. and even before they are teen-agers.

Clearly, we may have to cope with all kinds of situations as our children work to perfect their friend-selection processes. But at least we can take comfort in the fact that, by third grade or so, the boys are safely ensconced on one side of the room with the girls on the other. We do have a while before we have to worry about contending with car dates. That doesn't mean that the children aren't playing the game though. It is just that they will be using different forms of communication for a few years.

"Mommmm," Becky whined on one of those days when I had drawn the shortest straw and had been selected volunteer school playground supervisor, "Michael pulled off my barrette and threw it into the boys' rest room." I went in and told Michael to give her back her barrette, and he did. No argument.

"That wasn't so bad," I told myself, but that was before I got back to the playground and heard my child complaining to the other girls about how awful Michael is. Her mouth was saying one thing, but her eyes were definitely saying something else. I know, because I remember the look all too well.

"She loved it," I sighed, and I knew another stage in my life as a parent had just begun.

Friendships and Christian Growth

Many factors can affect a child's Christian growth when he begins to function outside the home environment, at least in part because our world is changing so rapidly. And so, our children are out there somewhere conversing with a talking vending machine, while we are struggling with a computer that understands everything but us. A few weeks ago, a teen-ager from my church was even asked to breakdance at a friend's wedding. In my day, we sang solos.

While all these changes are going on around us, we are raising a generation of children who are spending much more time out in the world than did the generations before them. It would only make sense, then, for us to get used to the fact that a child in today's world is going to be meeting many different kinds of people every day, people with all sorts of value systems, people with different religious beliefs. Thus, Becky's first best friend at school was a little Jewish girl.

"Can't Lynn come to church with me on Sunday mornings?" Becky would beg. "She can cover her ears whenever Jesus is mentioned."

In a situation like that, I figured my parental task was to teach my child to respect and accept people who believe differently from us. Otherwise, the very Christian faith I was trying to teach her would lose much of its clout. And so, Lynn never went to church with us, but we took her to lots of ball games. Revis and I also used this time in Becky's life to take our daughter outside to see rainbows so that we could tell her the Old Testament story of how the rainbow first came to be—and talk to her about her Church School lessons and about the special place of the Hebrew people in God's Word.

Becky and her friends seemed to be learning and growing at top speed during their early childhood years. And yet, there were days when I would wonder if any of them were learning anything really important. "How am I ever going to get through to this child?" I would ask myself. "I'm trying to teach the Bible to a person who believes that a red pencil is worth a fight to the death." There were also days when I felt like screaming. (I later found out that screaming is a normal developmental stage for the mother of a grade-school child.)

I wanted so badly for my child to see that what is truly significant in life is not to have the biggest doll house on the block or win some drawing contest or star in the school play, but rather "to do justly, and to love mercy, and to walk humbly with thy God." Then I discovered a strange fact about children. Just when you feel most certain that your child's Christian education is a lost cause, the little darling will usually come up with a way to surprise you.

"You're going to hate me tomorrow, Becky," I said to her as I tucked her into bed the night before her sixth Easter Sunday. Then I went on to explain to her how lousy she would feel when I woke her up for the church sunrise service the next morning— and I told her that I understood. (On my own list, getting out of bed before 9:00 A.M. ranks about two slots below going in for root-canal work.)

"Why do we have to get up so early, Mommy?" she asked. "What happens on Easter Sunday?"

While I was answering her question, she fell asleep; and I assumed she wouldn't retain any of my Easter message. The next morning, bleary-eyed and irritable, I walked into my daughter's room. She jumped out of bed cheering and clapping.

"Jesus rised! Jesus rised!" she shouted as she hopped and skipped through the house—which is, of course, the only appropriate response to Easter Sunday, or to anything in life, for that matter.

Parting Tips

When your child is making friends . . .

—Encourage her growing individuality and independence. This may not keep an eight-year-old girl from begging for a pair of jeans that Janie's parents can afford and you can't, but it will probably keep her from dropping out of active life when she doesn't get them.

—Check to make sure you yourself are modeling good reactions to peer pressure. Whether you tell her or not, your child knows if getting the money for a car just like the Smiths' is more important to you than spending an afternoon at the beach with her.

—Don't fuss over her. If you do, she is likely to get the idea that the world revolves around her (which only her grandmother truly believes), and the first time she doesn't win the class Best-Pipe-Cleaner-Town Award could end up being unnecessarily devastating for her.

—Show her that you feel good about sharing your day with people. Organize a neighborhood volleyball game once in a while, or ask her if she would like to have a party for a few friends. (Outdoors, if possible!) Don't expect to have a spotless home until your child is at least fifty either. Even if she isn't particularly messy, her friends will be.

—Pray for her and for her friends—and remember that God is always with your child, even when you aren't.

3

Why Can't They Ever Behave in Public?

The Child's Behavioral Style

"Just as a father punishes a son he delights in to make him better, so the Lord corrects you."

—Proverbs 3:12, TLB

By the time children enter the early school years, they have already developed distinct personalities. However, few people get to know a child well enough to find out what that personality is. Most people figure it's simply not worth wading through the spilled milk and snake collections and bathroom humor to get there. And yet, understanding your child's personality can help you understand her behavioral style.

Who Is This Little Person?

Becky is often described as perky and talkative. I suppose that's a personality of sorts. At least I know it's true. For, on the very day she was born, the doctor told me she came out talking. I seldom tell this to anyone though, because, whenever I do, my dear husband always announces that Becky takes after her mother—which is, of course, a total fabrication.

Actually, I said only two words on the day my daughter was born. Or at least this is what I am told. All I remember is that the baby got turned around in the womb (looking for someone to have a conversation with, no doubt), and I ended up undergoing

41

an emergency C-section and welcoming my daughter into the world with a groggy comment that sounded a lot like, "Dumb kid!"

By the time Becky had turned five, I had long since ceased thinking of her as a dumb kid. Indeed, on many occasions, I found her to be too smart for her own good.

The behavioral style of a five-year old child is probably most influenced by the fact that he can now hop, skip, climb, and do just about anything that leaves scuff marks—scuff marks on floors, on shoes, and everywhere else imaginable. One time when an interior designer asked me if I had furniture of a particular period in my home, I replied "My house is early scuff mark."

It's one thing for our homes to bear our children's marks, but it's something else entirely when we learn that the world at large does not escape their distinctive touch. What mother hasn't experienced those moments when her child's behavior in public causes her to wish the floor would conveniently open and swallow both her and her child.

"Having a daughter who jumps out from behind walls at home is one thing," sighed my friend Katie, "but last week Carolyn jumped out from behind a wall at the bank and sent three tellers straight to the burglar alarm."

I once read that a five-year-old has an intense desire to please his parents. I tried to hold onto that thought when my own daughter turned five, but I soon found out that having a child who aims to please is still about ten light years away from having a home that is peaceful and well organized.

I never had a lot of trouble living with the "flowers" Becky picked from my vegetable garden or even the no-bake cookies that tasted like they were made out of birdseed. But when my child went public with her questionable behavior, when she began to track her mud into the local art museum, I decided to seek out some advice from my friends.

"I can't help you," my friend Mary shook her head. "When Terry turned five, he was big on setting the table. But one night he couldn't find the paper napkins, so he strung three rolls of toilet paper from the bathroom to the kitchen and draped the table in them."

"I think you just have to take a deep breath and wait it out," my friend Sharon advised. "I'll never forget the Christmas dinner

Tommy decided to help prepare. He secretly tucked an unopened can of green peas into the oven with the turkey right before we all left for church, and you might say that year's feast ended up being garnished with green peas—as did our carpet, our staircase, and our dining room furniture."

Do They Really Have to Behave Like That?

Most psychologists agree that half of what a person learns in a whole lifetime is learned by age five. This includes basic survival skills, whom to trust and whom not to trust, how to manipulate and get one's way, and how to tell "white lies."

"My mother says I used to tell her the most incredible stories when I was little," a friend once admitted, "and I would tell them with great seriousness too, like, 'No, Mommy, I really didn't draw that picture of Raggedy Ann on the wall; the dog did it.' "

In recent years, many studies have been conducted that involve correlating childhood behavior to family birth order. Thus, we now know that first-born children are more likely to tow the line and accept the family guidelines and that second-born children might have an easier time making friends. Middle children are supposed to be more easygoing, while the youngest in the family often displays more creativity.

Add to this kind of information a few facts about the juvenile personality characteristics dependent upon age, and you could conceivably find out more about the behavioral style of your offspring than you ever really wanted to know. Take, for instance, the fact that a six-year-old, partly because she is suddenly expected to sit still so much of the day, is sometimes confused and unsure of herself and is more than capable of throwing a temper tantrum or getting into a fight without evidence of provocation. At this age, the child is also trying to cope with a number of school experiences that the parents know little about.

I understand all of this now, but I certainly over-reacted the night my daughter started calling a neighborhood friend a dipstick (that week's euphemism for "jerk") for no apparent reason. How was I to know that one second-grade class at school had been mercilessly teasing the other second-grade class because the former had learned how to write a "cursive I" first? The other kid knew perfectly well what he was doing though. He merely had to turn the corners of his mouth up into an evil, albeit toothless, grin, drop the magic words "cursive I," and then sit back and wait to reel in the gory details to tell his classmates at school the following day.

In many areas of childhood behavior, I have been even less perceptive than that. Take the area of thumb sucking, for example. I was sure the other children would tease that particular habit out of my child the minute she started school. But that was before I had occasion to visit my daughter's kindergarten classroom and look into the faces of twenty-five contented little cherubs—every one of whom had a thumb stuck in his or her mouth.

Then there is the issue of self-image. How much does a child's self-esteem, or lack of it, affect his behavioral style? The six-year-old who is afraid he can't live up to anyone's expectations . . . the seven-year-old who insists he is always left out of everything . . . the eight-year-old who is excessively critical—both of himself and of the people around him.

"At one point in my growing up years, I was in contention for an important award," a friend once explained. "I was the one who deserved the award too; but, when the judges interviewed me, I ruined my chances by telling why the other two contenders had more experience and ability than me." This woman is still struggling with her feelings of low self-esteem. Recently, she signed up for an assertiveness-training course because of it.

"How's the new class going?" I asked her last week at the supermarket.

"Terrible," she groaned. "I'm flunking it because I keep getting up and giving my seat to other people and moving to the back of the room."

Overcoming early feelings of self-doubt can be a very difficult task. That is why a child so desperately needs to be given an unconditional (regardless of report cards) kind of love. I once heard a speaker insist that a person needs four hugs a day to survive, eight for maintenance, and twelve for growth.

Praise is another self-doubt deterrent. A child needs to be praised for his good behavior. Granted, sometimes you have to look hard to find something that's praiseworthy. A case in point: One mother finally had to praise her son for hitting three people with a supermarket cart. Why? Because he mowed down eight people the week before.

We need to be aware of one more element as we attempt to evaluate our children's individual behavioral styles. That element is hero worship. By the time a child is attending grade school, he has begun to choose his heroes—scout leaders, school teachers, soccer coaches. And, most of us are acquainted with at least one potential artist, writer, or musician who completely buried both his talent and his outgoing personality because one of his childhood heroes refused to affirm him. Obviously, it would be difficult, if not impossible, to heal the scars left from an experience like that.

Go Directly to Your Room—Do Not Pass Go— Do Not Collect $200

I read a lot of books on child discipline when I was pregnant with Becky. Probably because I was afraid I wouldn't be able to discipline her correctly. Even now, there are days when I'm still not sure. And I suspect I am not the only one who feels that way.

"How do you get your children to behave?" I began asking other parents shortly after I became one. Most of them looked at me suspiciously, clearly wondering if I were naive enough to honestly believe I might be able to accomplish such a feat. Then, most likely out of a sense of pity, they began telling me the things that "sometimes" work for them.

"You have to be flexible," one parent advised. "For example, I was always dead set against giving material rewards; and, when Grandma promised Carrie a doll if she would stop sucking her thumb, I was furious. The trouble is, it worked. What can I say?"

"Appealing to the pocketbook usually works for me," a second parent explained. This parent scoops up the toys that her child has refused to put away and charges the child money to get the toys back.

"You have to be willing to follow through with your threats," warned a third parent, who once believed in counting to five and then spanking on the spot—until the day he found himself counting in the middle of a church worship service. This man is one among many parents who are still searching for the perfect mode of discipline, one among many parents who don't always get it right.

"I'll never forget the day Jackie told me that one of her neighbor-hood playmates was grounded," my friend Billie lamented. " 'What's grounded, Mommy?' she asked me; and, before I could catch myself, I heard myself saying, 'You know when we tell you if you do something bad you won't get to play with Becky? Well, they really do it over there at her house.' "

I can easily identify with such an experience. For, I almost got myself into a mess like that one Christmas. Exhausted and frustrated with my daughter's inability to go to sleep on Christmas Eve night, I blurted out the forbidden words: "If you don't go to sleep, you won't get any toys. I can promise you that!"

"How unfeeling can you be?" I later chided myself. After all, hadn't I dropped by my church's day nursery that afternoon and seen at least forty-five children spending their nap time sitting rigidly on their cots, wide-eyed, blankets stuffed in their mouths, ready to spring? And hadn't I talked to friends that very day and listened to them say things like, "Do you know Andy began asking if he could go to bed at 11:30 this morning?" Couldn't I remember what Christmas Eve feels like when you are six years old? Then I began to panic. . . . What if she doesn't go to sleep and I have to follow through with my threat? What in the world am I going to do with all this stuff?

Luckily, Mr. Sandman finally did get me out of that one; but I have since been very careful to avoid making idle threats in front of my child. I'm also trying to do a better job of giving clear, articulate instructions. I started working on that last summer, when Becky and her friend Sara asked me if they could put on their swimsuits and shoot water pistols at each other. "Sure," I called from the kitchen, but I had no idea they meant they wanted to do this inside the house.

Other parents have found themselves in similar situations. One mother instructed her child to "Wear your coat!" so many times last winter that she ended up getting a call from the child's teacher asking if she had any idea why Sally refused to take off her coat in the classroom that day. Another parent gave such explicit instructions to her son to hang his new jacket neatly on a hanger at school that he ended up stuffing it into his desk because the school coat room had hooks instead of hangers.

Of course, as all parents know, there are some days when

you just can't win. You can't always do everything by the books either, even when you know the books are right. . . . "Are you going to kill me?" Becky asked me in fear and trembling the night she spilled Jell-O on the newly laid carpet. The fact that I shouldn't have been letting her eat Jell-O in the living room in the first place was not nearly enough to keep me from screaming, "Yes! Anyone who spills Jell-O on a new carpet doesn't deserve to live!"

"I thought you didn't believe in letting children play with guns," I remarked to a friend whose child was trying to put a toy bullet through my head.

"That was last year," she sighed. "Now it's anything to get through the day."

Children feel more secure when they have limits, when they are treated with fairness and consistency, when they are not (as Ephesians 6:4 reminds us) provoked to anger. Most of us have no trouble agreeing with all that because we see proof of it all around us.

A nursery school teacher told me about a little girl who was brought to school in the middle of winter in an unlined nylon jacket. Her parents said they let her wear it because she refused to wear anything else. "I see this sort of thing all the time," the teacher shook her head, "and children like that are crying out so clearly for a firm hand."

Many parents agree that even teen-age children want limits, though few teen-agers would ever admit it. One mother cited her fifteen-year-old daughter as a good example of this. The young girl, upon getting her mother's permission to renew an acquaintance with a boy from summer church camp, immediately cornered her mother with the question, "What happened to the rule that I couldn't date until sixteen?"

It helps to understand all of this. And yet, no matter how hard we try, we know there are still going to be those days when our children are going to behave in an absolutely impossible fashion. And our children know it too.

Several little bundles of joy from my own neighborhood were sitting on Becky's bed playing dolls the other day. I walked by the door just in time to hear one of them saying, "Yours can be the mommy doll, mine will be the daddy doll, and yours can be the kids." The one with the kid dolls quickly inquired, "Which one of my kids should be bad first?" I think life with kids is getting more complicated by the day.

Most five-year-old children are notorious show-offs, while most eight-year-olds have begun to resent parental authority. Thus, it would seem to follow that giving a five-year-old a minimum amount of attention for misbehavior would solve his problem. Then you would only have to learn how to compromise with the eight-year-old—asking, "What would you think of cleaning your room after we play softball?" for example, as opposed to, "If there is one pair of jeans on your floor tomorrow morning, we're selling the VCR!" If only that supposition were true.

The first two times I tried the soft-sell approach to messy rooms, it worked perfectly. The third time, I ended up in the emergency room of the local hospital with an old style Barbie doll stand stuck straight through the middle of my foot.

"Ah, the malevolent Barbie doll stand," my doctor chuckled.

"When you're sitting on a table with a hole in your foot, the last thing you need is a doctor who is a comedian," I scowled.

Becky looked so contrite after that experience that I am sure she believed she was sorrier than I was about the whole thing. But she was wrong. She wasn't the one who had to get the tetanus shot. In fact, I figured her great burden of guilt would wear off even before the pain from the shot did. So, I decided I'd better take away a few of her privileges to strengthen the impact. She didn't like that idea at all. "At least I can honestly say it hurts me more than it does you this time," I said, rubbing my arm; but she didn't even have the decency to smile.

Discipline: In the Trenches

Through the years I've picked up some pretty good tips on how to discipline children. And, more often than not, they seem to work. For example, one parent told me that all children must be treated as individuals, that different things work for different kids. She originally got this idea from the story of the prodigal son, when the elder son began questioning the seemingly preferential treatment being given to his brother.

The same parent, a mother of five, has often advised me to consider my rules carefully and to remember that some things are simply not worth arguing about—For instance, a child's off-color story that can best be handled with a nonchalant, "That's not a good joke". . . or a flippant remark that may be a cover-up for the child's real feelings.

"Mom, Jenny and I want to have a private talk on the telephone," Becky once declared. "Would you please go to your room now?" I certainly didn't bow my head and shuffle obediently off to another room on that occasion, but I didn't start ranting and raving about having been there to wipe my child's bottom long before she knew what a telephone was, either. Instead, I did some thinking about how I was going to handle my child's very real need for privacy. Only three weeks before, she had made an elaborate sign for her bedroom door. "Don't come in; no company too," it read. I knew she was trying to tell me something.

And so, I tried to tread more softly through Becky's private zones after that. I bought her a diary and promised never to look for the key; and I began searching for ways to let her know how much I respect her right, as a unique human being, to be herself. One of a kind.

Many parents have warned me that the "everybody's doing it" stage, a stage which has a definite impact on behavior, makes its appearance long before puberty. One of them even told me how to handle it. "I always said to my child, 'You're not everybody; you are my child, my gift from God,' " this mother explained. Then she continued, "Have you ever watched a baby tear open a present? Even a one-year-old knows that a gift is something special, and everyone wants to feel special."

This woman's children were required to live by a set of rules that would be considered very strict by today's standards. And yet, she insists that those rules made her children feel loved. She points to two examples of this—the fact that young people have asked to come home with her children so they could spend their college holidays with a caring family and the fact that she recently overheard her daughter say to her own children, "But you are not everybody; you are my gifts from God."

I firmly believe we can learn a lot about discipline from talking with other parents, as long as we remember that each child is an individual and must be treated as such and as long as we remember that some tactics will work perfectly in one family and flop miserably in another. I try to remember this whenever a generally accepted method of discipline—for example, letting the child help devise the penalties for his crimes—isn't working for me.

"What do you think we should do to punish you for this?" I asked Becky when she was in first grade and had broken a flower vase during a temper tantrum. The article I had read promised me that if I said these words in a cool, controlled parental tone of voice, I would be given suggested punishments that would be so severe I would simply have to sift through them, end up telling my child I would only make her wash ten loads of laundry this time, and come out smelling like a rose.

"Well, Mommy," Becky replied after much thought, "I think you should punish me by putting my picture face down on the dresser for two days."

I never did much better in the area of spanking either. Most of my friends do spank, but only when it's "absolutely necessary." I was never sure what "absolutely necessary" meant. To some it seemed to mean hearing the child say a word that is off limits, while to others it was reserved for those times when (and this really did happen) you see your child tie the family dog to his tricycle and allow Rover to pull him out in front of an eighteen-wheeler.

The only time I actually felt like spanking Becky was the day she crawled, unseen, onto the back of a bathroom scale I was standing on and caused the needle to register an extra seven pounds. She was too young to spank at the time though, and nothing else she ever did seemed so bad in comparison.

I don't spank anyone else's children either. I guess I've just heard too many war stories told by parents who have tried to teach someone else's child a lesson. In fact, I always bend over backwards never to correct any of Becky's friends, though I've had to work hard, on occasion, to control the urge. Like that day when we were entertaining guests for dinner, and one of the younger children began burping after the meal.

"That's impolite!" Becky screeched, in her typically tactful way.

"Did you know that, in some countries, it is considered a great compliment to the host to burp after a meal?" I softly reprimanded her.

"Really?" she responded, "then they'd sure like the new kid

who got transferred into our class at school last week, because he burps *before* meals."

Rebuked by God

Clearly, disciplining your child can be both a complex and a controversial issue. There is a lot of trial and error involved. And yet, you must never give up. For, from a parent who disciplines fairly and well, a child learns so much about his heavenly Father.

When you love and forgive your child, the child is more likely to trust God to do the same. When you care what happens to your child, you are helping to teach God's lesson of the lilies of the field. . . . "I'm going to leave my Cabbage Patch Kids with Mrs. Borland when I go on our trip," Becky announced, "and I'm going to leave lots of rules for them to follow so nothing bad will happen to them."

We ended up depositing the dolls at the home of our family friends with a long list of rules that covered everything from nutritional advice ("They have to eat Brussels sprouts at every meal, or they won't get a Snickers bar again until they are seventeen years old") to bedtime instructions ("They can watch TV until 7:30, but no R ratings"). I took this as a positive sign that my child understood she has rules because her parents love her. Still, I figured I shouldn't dare hope that her understanding would extend to the idea that saying no to a school-night slumber party or taking away a toy when her bed doesn't get made might also be for her own good. Maybe someday, though.

"If two kids were playing in the middle of the street," one minister explained to his congregation, "and the father of one of them came along, he would pull them both out of the street; but there is only one he would really discipline." Then the minister began talking about Hebrews 12:6, and about the fact that a true child of God can expect to have his hand slapped from time to time.

Of course, this doesn't mean that all the bad things that happen to us on earth are punishments for our wrongs. After all, the Bible makes it clear that bad times come to both the just and the unjust. That is why I believe it is most important to hang onto the image of a heavenly Father who loves us perfectly, the image of a God who lets us learn by making mistakes, a God who pulls us out of the murk and helps us try again.

God's example of parental guidance should challenge us as parents to be there for our families, to concentrate on our children's good qualities, and to discipline out of love. I realize that children have individual behavioral styles that can frustrate even the best of parents; but, believe it or not, there *will* be those days when your child will behave like a perfect little angel. Enjoy it while it lasts, for I'm convinced that all children have an unwritten group pact by which they live—*they have all agreed never to be that good in public!*

Parting Tips

When it's time to think about your child's behavior . . .

—Make sure you know him as well as possible. Consider his strengths, his weaknesses, his basic personality. Look closely. It's difficult to detect a personality in someone who has an attention span of only ten seconds.

—Work on finding ways to build up his self-image—and don't forget that your own self-image has a direct effect on his. All of this takes work though. Even the seemingly routine task of spending time answering a child's questions takes on new significance when you read *Encyclopedia Brown's Record Book of Weird and Wonderful Facts* and find out that the average preschooler asks 437 questions a day.

—Surround him with unconditional love. And remember that grandparents are generally fantastic at giving it. If your family doesn't live nearby, don't hesitate to look around for some substitute grandparents. Mobility has invaded twentieth-century life to such an extent that more and more of us are finding ourselves separated by great distance from the comfort and support of family. (When Becky was two, she thought Grandma was a telephone.)

—Choose your style of discipline carefully, and discuss it with your spouse. Nothing is worse than saying to a child, "Wait until your dad gets home," and then forgetting what the kid did wrong by the time he does.

—When life gets really tough, remind yourself that people grow from hardship—and raising children can often qualify as pretty extreme hardship.

4

Behind the Freckles

Emotional Development

"Guard your heart more than any treasure, for it is the source of all life."

Proverbs 4:23, NEB

"There has always been a basic assumption in our society," according to Dr. Kenneth Story, director of an Ohio pastoral counseling center, "that children are not little people, but are, rather, yard apes, carpet creepers, second-class citizens." Dr. Story emphasizes his point with such facts as (1) until this century, many children were forced to work in factories, (2) although children have always been abused, only in the last few years have children's rights been in vogue, and (3) "children should be seen and not heard" is still one of the best known sayings in America.

Do we really believe that children are not as important as big people? Do we think, deep down inside, that no one under the age of twenty-one is able to say anything worth hearing or to make any kind of significant contribution to society?

Do Children Have Feelings, Too?

I am interested in my Becky's feelings and needs. I really am. It's just that every time I try to talk to her about them, I always come away from the conversation wondering what we actually said. Take for example the following conversations:

"And how did you feel when Amy beat you in the relay race at school today, Becky?"

"I felt thirsty enough to drink a glass of bugs."

"That's not exactly what I meant, dear; and, besides, you mean bug juice."

"Are you kidding? I wouldn't drink bug juice!"

* * *

"But what did you feel like when Michael asked you to be his girl friend?"

"Okay, I guess."

"Did you tell him yes or no?"

"I told him yes, but I lied."

Maybe the key to success in all this is found in remembering that a child's feelings and emotions are going to be determined, at least in part, by the stage he is in at the time. Take the seven-year-old, for example. According to studies done at the Gesell Institute of Human Development, most seven-year-olds are absolutely paranoid. They spend most of their time saying things like, "The teacher isn't my friend," or, "Why do I have all the bad luck?" Citing these studies, writer Veronica Thomas concludes, "About the best thing to be said of a seven-year-old is that he will become eight—eventually."[1]

Thus, although it is necessary for children to feel free to express their emotions to their parents, it is also necessary for the parents to understand that those feelings may not always have a basis in fact. Sometimes even the language Becky uses to express her feelings doesn't appear to have much basis in fact.

"I'm so cold out here," she once informed me. "I think I'll go inside and hot off." Frequently, after a day of conversing with this child and her equally incomprehensible friends, I spend the evening trying to figure out what I have really done all day.

"The only thing I learned today," I often tell Revis, "is that Becky would be perfect for the job of TV sitcom writer."

No doubt about it. Understanding your children's feelings is not an easy task. Of course, those parents who understand their children's likes and dislikes do seem to be ahead of the game. Take my friend Paula, for example. She knows her youngest son pretty well. "Jamie would sleep in his baseball uniform if we would let him," she once told me.

"That's for sure," added Jamie's older brother, Andy, "and if one of his friends were lying dead on the ground, Jamie would walk up to the kid and say, 'Hey, do you want to play ball?'"

Some children's likes and dislikes are not quite so evident, but discovering more about them is a task that is generally well worth the effort involved. Especially when the children begin demonstrating a need for independence.

Veronica Meyer, an Ohio day-nursery director, contends that families are fragmented today because too many of them don't see themselves as a unit. "Parents and children set themselves in conflict situations," she maintains, "and parents constantly struggle for power instead of admitting that their children actually do need increasing amounts of control and power over themselves and over their environments."

Mrs. Meyer believes that much of the trouble could be eliminated if parents would realize the importance of providing challenging, but possible, tasks for their children. She does this in her day nursery with art materials, glue, anything that the child can change around or take apart and put back together, anything that gives the child a feeling of mastery over his environment.

Most authorities also advise allowing children to make choices whenever possible. The wisest ones advise parents to make sure that both of the choices offered are acceptable choices. For example, I would feel very comfortable saying to my child, "Would you rather clean your room before or after lunch?" I would feel much less comfortable saying, "Would you rather go to the swimming pool with Joannie or to the zoo with Francine and her mother (neither of whom appear to have the ability to make it to the zoo and back in one piece)?" So I don't say that. Besides, I figure I am old enough to outsmart an eight-year-old, at least some of the time.

Welcome to Carpool City

"I liked kindergarten when I was five because I was 'into' toys," Becky announced when she had completed her first week of first grade, "but I like first grade now because I'm 'into' homework." It was my first indication that she felt it important for me to see that she was growing up.

After that, Becky's need for independence began to reveal itself in all sorts of ways. She started asking for a private table at McDonald's, for instance; and she started using the words, *"I can do it myself"* almost as often as she used the word *"gross."* She also started getting more involved in outside activities and spending more time with friends. I soon found out that she was not the only six-year-old who was 'into' independence.

"Ben spent his first night away from home last weekend," my friend Linda told me, "and I was a basket case."

"Did he have a lot of trouble?" I inquired sympathetically.

"No," Linda replied, "that was the worst part. He didn't ask for me once!"

Even children need their own space. Perhaps especially children. They need to be allowed to do things for themselves. "The greatest mistake I made as a parent," one mother said, "was to love my children too fiercely—and protect them too often." This woman explained that she would see mean little bullies in the neighborhood, the kind of kids who put nonpoisonous spiders in little girls' lunch boxes only because they can't find any poisonous ones; and she would decide she just couldn't let her children fight battles like that, so she would fight their battles for them. "When my children went beyond my reach," she concluded, "they were hurt much more often than they would have been if I had let them fight their own fights."

Many parents, in retrospect, feel the same way. They say they wouldn't hover so much if they had it to do over. But the temptation to run interference for one's children is something that seems to be in a parent's blood. "Let Mommy kiss it and make it better," we say, knowing full well that we have no real healing capacities and that the most we are going to do with our kisses is spread a few more germs around.

Of course, children do need to know their parents are there for them—supporting them, believing in them, loving them. A counselor friend once told me that children know if they're unwanted from hour one, and if they are still unwanted by age five, they will bear the open wounds forever.

"They don't ever stop needing to know we care," a mother of teen-agers advised me. "I'll never forget the day one of mine said to me, 'Mom, you can't keep me from falling anymore, so you're going to have to stop trying, but I wouldn't mind if you'd still be willing to wait around with the Band-Aids.'"

And yet, there comes a time (or perhaps, many times along the way) when we must let go. First, we have to let go of the bicycle, with smiles of confidence on our faces, while visions of hospital emergency rooms and secondary infections run through our minds. Eventually, we have to let go of the car keys, and pretend that we really do trust our lives to a person who is wearing a Carburetors-Are-My-Life T-shirt.

In many ways, it's not easy for us to see our children grow up, to silently accept the fact that we have no right to control their thoughts and feelings, to encourage them to try new things even though we remember the messes we have had to bail them out of in the past.

Last year, Becky decided she was ready to walk to a friend's house by herself. The friend only lived a few blocks away, but I hid behind a tree and watched her cross the streets anyway. What I saw was a lesson in parenting that I will never forget. My daughter skipped and sang all the way to her destination, clearly intoxicated by her new freedom. Openly and joyfully embracing a world over which she finally had some control. It was a sight that was thrilling to see.

On my way home, I tried to remember what it felt like to be out there on my own for the first time. Frightening, yes; but I was so ecstatic. It was right, and it was good—the way God meant for it to be. And then I thought of a childhood friend who never quite made it out into the world. She had parents who said to her every time she went out of the door, "We always hate to see you leave because, with all the bad things happening in the world, we always wonder if this will be the last time we will ever see you."

I know I have to let go more often, but I still have those days when I wonder how I am ever going to accept my child's bid for independence with dignity and grace. Like that day last week when I found a red plastic egg on my doorstep. Inside the egg was a crumpled note scrawled by one of my daughter's fellow classmates. "I love you Becky, Christopher," it read. The little boy had chosen red because it was three weeks after Valentine's Day and an egg because it was three weeks before Easter. Not bad for a lovesick second grader.

At first, I looked at this experience as a personal rejection, one more step in Becky's growing up—and away—process. But then I decided I was being too sensitive, not to mention silly. Christopher can't even write in cursive yet. And, knowing my daughter, I hardly think I'm in danger of losing her to any boy who hasn't yet learned how to sign a check.

Eventually, I settled on a different approach. I told myself that an eight-year-old continues to need her mom, in many ways, so the grade-school years are just too soon to worry about empty-nest syndrome. Most parents of school-age children agree, particularly those parents who know what it's like to work with one child in preparation for welcoming a new one into the fold.

But I'd Rather Have a Puppy

"Mother," my friend's eighteen-year-old daughter said to her one day, "do you remember the chocolate ear game you used to play with Donnie and me when you tucked us into bed?" She didn't, so her daughter continued. "You used to say, 'Okay, who has the chocolate ear tonight?' And then you would kiss our ears to find out."

"Oh yes," the mother replied, still not sure she remembered.

"Donnie always seemed to have the chocolate ear," the young woman sighed, "and I always had to settle for strawberry—and I used to lie awake at night and wonder why it could never be me." The mother was astonished. "It took me a long time to get over that, Mom," the daughter disclosed, "a very long time."

A child's emotions can run rampant when he is faced with the prospect of learning how to live with a sibling. And why wouldn't this be true? After all, in most cases the child is facing the biggest adjustment he has had to make in life so far. He knows he is going to lose some of the status he enjoyed as the only kid around. There is bound to be some resulting jealousy and competition.

Most parents feel that it helps to prepare the older child for his new role, to involve him in various aspects of new baby care, even to enroll him in a hospital sibling class. Such parents advise making the older child an integral part of the younger sibling's life. They warn against going overboard either by neglecting the baby or by tending to the younger child mainly when the older one is not around. And yet, the fights for parental attention seem to be very difficult to avoid.

One of my friends has a child who was extremely hurt when her parents refused to name the new baby Strawberry Shortcake. Another child always insisted that his brother picked on him for no reason and begged his father to tell Jesus about it because "He will probably tell Santa Claus." A third child was toilet trained very late because she wanted to go to the bathroom like her twin brother. Whenever her mother sat her down on the toilet, she popped back up and stood in front of it. These are not unusual kinds of stories. In fact, in some homes, family life is totally disrupted by the presence of sibling rivalry.

One article I read suggested that those of us who are parents of more than one child would be better off not simply answering the inevitable question, "Which one of us do you love best?" with the expected, but not very satisfying, "I love you both the same." Rather, writer Lisa W. Strick believes we should try to understand each child's individual need to feel special. We should spend time alone with each child and tell each child, during those times, what we especially like about him. At the very least, most people agree that it is essential to avoid useless comparisons and to avoid the practice of taking sides.

"Mommy, Julie hit me with her headphones again," one sibling bawls. (Years ago, it used to be "Julie hit me with her rag doll.") The majority of parents believe the wisest thing to do in a case like this is to remember that both sides are usually at fault whenever there is an argument between children—and to separate the siblings until they can get along together again (1999, perhaps). While the children are young, it doesn't hurt to put some distance between them at the dinner table, too. (About three city blocks would be preferable.)

Some parents solve dinner table squabbles by sending the offending parties to their rooms and making them wait to eat dinner until after everyone else is done. This accomplishes two purposes. It prevents moms from losing a good night's sleep because they are sure their children will starve to death by morning; and it teaches the children a lesson, since nothing takes the fun out of a good fight quicker than enforced solitude. Still, as is true with almost everything in life, once will probably not be nearly enough. And many parents, who have remained patient for years, have told me they are planning to nominate themselves as parents of the year when their children finally do become friends.

One pastoral counselor I know, when working with parents whose children are displaying hostile behavior toward their siblings, always asks those families about their bedtime rituals. Generally, he finds that the older child is being given less attention at bedtime due to the birth of the younger child. And, he often finds that something as simple as adding that extra story back into the older child's bedtime ritual is enough to get the entire family organization back to normal.

His advice to parents is that first you have to accept the fact that the message your child is acting out through misbehavior might be a legitimate message, and then you have to understand that bedtime is the time when a child is most open, most vulnerable, and least able to cope with his fears. This is true, of course, whether the child has siblings or not.

Please Don't Turn the Light Off, Mommy

When a child goes to sleep at night, he has to close his eyes and trust his environment. He has to gamble that everything will be there in the morning. That is why feeling safe is a prerequisite to sleeping well. It is why children always seem to wait until bedtime to ask their parents why the goldfish died.

I have frequently done a lousy job of handling Becky's bedtime problems. I know I have. One night, for example, when she was afraid of some monster she had seen on a billboard, I tried telling her how silly she was being. I told her that some kids get so worked up about make-believe monsters they end up convincing themselves that there are real monsters hiding under their beds waiting to chop their feet off.

That would show her how ridiculous the whole thing was, I figured; but I soon found out I couldn't have been more wrong. As it turned out, I had to bribe my child with the promise of a Michael Jackson album just to get her to put her feet down on the bedroom floor after that.

I had forgotten that children's fears are never very rational. This doesn't make them seem less real, however. One Fourth of July, in fact, Becky was so frightened by the noise of the fireworks that she started going into hysterics over just about any halfway similar sound. It was pretty embarrassing with Becky running for cover every time someone closed a car door, or diving

under a ticket booth because of the sound of corn popping in
a movie theater. If you don't understand why this is embarrassing,
try defending the sanity of a child like that to a middle-aged,
childless couple who are merely looking for a peaceful night at
the cinema.

Young children can be afraid of just about anything—the dog
next door, a test at school, even a flushing toilet. They are also
afraid of losing their parents. ("Do you think Daddy's been adult-
napped?" Becky sometimes asks me when Revis is late getting
home from work.) Occasionally, these fears can be traced to specific events, as in the case of one friend of mine who grew up
afraid of lightning. (She believes it is because, as a child, she
was instructed to stop playing on the floor and sit on the couch
with her hands folded during thunderstorms.) Other times, no
one can be sure where a child's fears come from. It is the same
with nightmares.

According to one psychological study, at least two-thirds of
youngsters' dreams are of the disturbing variety. We tend to play
this down with our children, but I can certainly remember the
last time I woke up in a cold sweat—and how scary a dream
truly can be. And yet, this doesn't mean that I am going to give
up my own good night's sleep to sit by my child's bed and be
her teddy bear every night. It doesn't mean I'm going to give
up something that's even more fun than a restful night to spend
the best years of my life sleeping three to a bed either.

I'm usually fairly patient through the "I forgot to brush my
teeth and go to the bathroom" ploy, and even during the "It's
too hot/too cold" fiasco. But when Becky starts the "I want another drink" stall, my patience begins to fray at the edges. Her
next words are usually, "But none of my friends go to bed at
9:00."

"I know," I always say. "All of your friends go to bed at 8:30."
This is when my child starts mumbling something about my talking
to her friends' mothers too often, and then goes back to the
brushing teeth line again (just in case I've forgotten she has already
gotten up once for that).

I've tried getting a bigger night light, and I've tried starting
the countdown to bedtime so early that Perry Como could move
fast enough to get everything done before zero hour. I've also
tried letting my child read or listen to the radio. I've always put

her to bed with a happy, light attitude, too; and I've spent lots of time assuring her that all of her feelings are normal (even when I have my doubts). I've finally decided there is no way to get my daughter to really enjoy lights out.

Last night was a particularly bad one. Revis and I sat slumped in separate chairs after it was all over and started talking about it.

"Do you think most parents actually put their children to bed at 7:30 and spend the rest of the night enjoying passionate romps in the hay together?" I asked.

"From the looks of most of them, I doubt it," he answered.

"Well, that's some consolation," I sighed.

"Did you know that Rachel once said to Jacob, 'Give me children or I shall die?' " he continued, trying to inject a little of his ministerial humor into the conversation.

"She must have meant something different," I scowled. "But just don't get any ideas about being sent off to some handmaid."

Must Fears of Dark Lead to Fears of Death?

Although young children have many different kinds of fears, most of them will talk about death very openly and honestly. It is important that they be encouraged to do so, partly because they just might have it figured out all wrong.

I once read an article in which writer Bill Adler asked children to comment on the subject of death. One eight-year-old described the experience this way: "When you die, they bury you in the ground and your soul goes to heaven, but your body can't go to heaven because it's too crowded up there already."

Another eight-year-old had similar ideas. "When you die," she explained, "they put you in a box and bury you in the ground because you don't look too good."

Many parents are hesitant to talk with their children about death; it is a difficult subject to discuss, especially since most adults aren't sure that they understand it all themselves. I was raised in an era when children were "protected" from death, left at home to play while everyone went to say good-bye to Grandpa.

An elderly friend of ours died when Becky was six years old. She had nicknamed him Purple Pieman and had played with him often. She asked if she could go to the funeral home. Revis and I sought advice from a local funeral director.

"By all means take her," he told us. "It will be much better this way than if it were a grandparent the first time." Then he added, "Don't be surprised if she understands it all better than you do though."

He was absolutely right. Becky, with her childlike faith in God, took the attitude of "Certainly people die when they get old; that's the way life is, and there is no doubt whatsoever that our friend could be anywhere else but in the presence of almighty God at this very moment."

Becky asked us that day why the man didn't look white and pale. ("That's just a body, Mommy. It isn't really Purple Pieman. He's with Jesus.") And she asked if the sunbeams she saw in the sky the day before were the beams God used to take Purple Pieman to heaven. After she left the funeral home, she told us she is glad Jesus lives in her heart because now Purple Pieman can live in her heart too since he's with Jesus.

Revis and I learned a lot about life and death during that experience with Becky. And we gained a brand new understanding of the reason why Jesus told us that we must become like little children to enter the kingdom of heaven.

Other parents have also learned much from their children on similar occasions. Like my friend John, for example, whose first-grade son once asked him if you can take things to heaven with you. "No," John told the boy, "you can't take anything with you; but God will have everything you need in heaven, so you don't have to worry about it."

"You mean God will even have a left-handed catcher's mitt?" the son replied with great enthusiasm.

God knows how important the feelings of little children really are. And so does every parent who is not afraid to enter the complex, precious, and unique world of a child.

Parting Tips

When you are trying to understand your child's feelings . . .

—Don't hover. Let her go ahead and do a task herself. If you had someone following you around picking up your clothes, you probably wouldn't ever bend down again either.

—Brush up on your family communication skills. Ask your child to tell you something she did at school that day. If you have trouble getting her to talk, try talking to her at bedtime. She will be willing to discuss anything in order to postpone going to sleep.

—Plan individual activities with each of your children. Think back to what it felt like to have Mom or Dad all to yourself for a whole day when you were in grade school. You might even be able to get by with doing something that doesn't involve cartoons or lollipops if your child is excited enough about being with you.

—When she begins to show her independent streak, be sure she remembers her basic safety rules. Emphasize the importance of knowing one's name, address, phone number, and rules about strangers. It's worth taking a chance that your child might become a little less trusting for a while. (Once, Becky started yelling at Revis because he had nodded at a "stranger" in a forest ranger uniform during a hike through the woods.)

—Teach her that God created her with feelings and emotions, and teach her that God never created anything that wasn't very, very special.

5

Childhood Pressure Cookers

The Child and Stress

"He who brings trouble on his family inherits the wind."
—Proverbs 11:29, NEB

Recently, I ran across a newspaper article about a children's telephone hotline in the Chicago area. In 1984, that hotline received more than 18,000 calls; and the people who took those calls believe the number would have doubled if they'd had more lines. The children who made the calls talked about everything from report cards to lost pets to divorce to thoughts of prostitution and suicide. Most of them, according to the article, were lonely and just wanted someone to talk to.

Stress Among Our Babies

There is a lot of stress among today's children, and you can see it everywhere. The tough little boy who uses his fists to prove he isn't scared to go home to an empty house every day. The former "A" student who is too worried about the outcome of her parents' next fight to do her homework. And have you noticed how few kids ever calm down long enough to learn how to whisper? "My child's motto in life," explained one frustrated parent, "is 'If you're not screaming, you're whispering.'"

Not only are today's children reacting to stress, but they are often using their reactions to drive their parents nuts . . . "I wish

I had Mr. and Mrs. Johnson for parents," my friend's daughter yelled at the end of one of her regularly scheduled fits.

"Why don't you go over and ask them?" the mother yelled back, mostly because she was at the end of her day's rope. "Maybe they will take you."

We may laugh at this mother's frustration, but childhood experts agree that stress in children is a growing concern.

• Dr. Barbara Kuczen, professor of early childhood education at Chicago State University, says that one out of ten children suffers from emotional or mental illness and that many young children are worried about such things as nuclear war.

• Dr. Steven Stack, associate professor of sociology at Pennsylvania State University, thinks that the three factors responsible for the huge increase in youth suicides in the last twenty years are declining church attendance, increase in unemployment among young people, and increase in broken homes.

• Dr. David Elkind, professor of child study at Tufts University in Massachusetts, explained in a recent newspaper interview that he believes the problems we are seeing with drug and alcohol abuse, psychological difficulties, crime, and even suicide among the young are a direct result of children being rushed into adulthood before they are prepared for it.

When I was a kid, I thought guns were only used by Matt Dillon and G.I. Joe, and my parents certainly never talked about any problems in front of me. I didn't know anyone who had ever been divorced either, and my sexual curiosity had to be assuaged by watching Lucy and Desi peck each other on the cheek at bedtime. My parents lived by the rule "A naive child is a happy child." I must have been one of the happiest.

Perhaps in some ways, I was too naive. Perhaps it is a good thing that I can't think of too many children who know how to blush anymore. Perhaps it is better to be like the young girl down the street, whose friend once visited her home and said to her, in great amazement, "You mean you live with both of your real parents?" At least that girl will know what odds she is going to have to face out there.

And yet, Dr. Elkind insists that studies prove that children who are exposed to everything early in life, children who are "deprived of the protected period of time they need to develop a strong sense of self," are *not* better prepared to be productive citizens.

"A good experience is the best preparation for a bad experience," he explained, "not the opposite."

But the children I see around me continue to grow up at top speed, getting their false desires from television, their nervous stomachs from school tests, and their ideas for overly packed schedules from Mom and Dad who forgot what roses smell like a long time ago. All of this at an age when most of us were doing our fretting over whether to spend the afternoon playing marbles or jumping rope.

Of the millions of today's children who have working mothers, as many as one-third of those children go unsupervised for long periods of time each day. Some of them have parents who carry around electronic paging devices so their children can check in with them from time to time—to see who's smearing peanut butter on whom, no doubt. Other children have checklists waiting for them at home each day, in the hopes of keeping them busy polishing their shoes instead of sliding down mud holes in them. But most of the unsupervised children in the world seem to end up at my house—making airplanes out of my checklists, and smearing peanut butter on me.

Children's nightmares used to be about green, scaly creatures who looked like something one of them might have drawn in a first grade art class. Now those nightmares are just as likely to be about nuclear war and annihilation of the human race.

"I don't think parents would have trouble understanding their children's feelings and stresses if they would find enough time to listen to their children and discover that they do have feelings," one teacher told me. Then she went on to add that all of a child's negative feelings are not caused by the changing world in which we live. "There are days when I feel grumpy," this woman explained, "so why shouldn't a child have the right to feel grumpy sometimes too?"

Stress in Pink Tights

I understand many of Becky's day-to-day stresses, probably because I share a lot of them with her, although I don't always do so willingly. . . . "Oh, I'm so happy; I feel like all my prayers have been answered," my mother cried the day I informed her that Becky had asked if she could take ballet lessons. I have the only mother in the world who set out, in vain, to have a child who would one day be an entertainer.

"Are you happy enough to pay for the lessons?" I asked her. "And the costumes and the shoes and the recital fees and the practice clothes?"

I guess my major problem with all this is not so much the fact that I finally talked my mother into letting me stop taking dance lessons only after I had put in ten miserable years at it, but more the idea that I have never been able to picture myself as a stage mother.

And so, I sit there, week after week, trying to make jokes with the other mothers. "Well, here comes our little herd of graceful calves, clopping down the stairs," I sometimes chuckle, usually mostly to myself. Once, when all the mothers were sitting around at a costume organizational meeting, I came up with what I thought was a really great line. "A Supermom would love this," I said, "and would probably even be baking coffee cakes for the next meeting." No one laughed, but one woman immediately started planning refreshments. It took me a long time to find out that stage mothers never get a good joke.

Of course, all of those mothers aren't of the stage variety. I did meet some new friends in that group, mothers to cry with while I try to whip up a costume fit for the Broadway stage— with a handful of discount remnants and a thirty-year-old sewing machine.

Whenever the tension begins to ease, recital time generally rolls around. Last year, the frustration level was about par for the course. A little daisy freaked out after the elastic under her chin had cut through three layers of skin. And a little poodle, who had been reminded by her mother so many times to pick up her tail (if it fell off) and continue dancing, picked up someone else's tail, thinking it was hers, and promptly got chased off the stage. They were small incidents, small incidents of the type that can add a few more stress points into the mix.

Easing the Crunch

Since just about any change in life, good or bad, can produce stress, there is no way to provide your children with a stress-free environment. In fact, their lives would be pretty shallow and boring if you could. You can, however, teach your children how to handle and use stress; and you can begin to do this with them at a very early age.

A parent should show his children love and encourage them to develop positive self-images and utilize good communication skills when teaching them how to cope with stress. Most people agree with that. But the question remains. How can we make sure we are on the right track?

My pastoral-counselor friend Kenneth Story suggests teaching your children impulse control. "Some parents teach their kids that people who are kicked have the right to kick back," he says, "but it is much better to teach your children that they do not have to give in and be victims of their own impulses." Dr. Story believes you can give your children this message in many ways, through behavior modification, appropriate disciplinary techniques, and, most significant of all, modeling.

"Trouble comes when Mom and Dad get totally freaked out over the TV news and start yelling, 'Oh my gosh! Oh my gosh! Look at that air pollution!' " continues Dr. Story, "or when the parents find out that a neighbor has accidentally pulled up one of their flowers, and they threaten to call the police." The approach you need to use in the home is one of calm, conversational problem-solving, not one of panic.

Being aware of the stress in a child's life and trying not to add any unnecessary extra stress also helps. This might include thinking twice before grounding a child whose time with his friends helps him relax and cope with his stress. Or being careful not to inadvertently heighten a child's fear of desertion, one of the most stressful thoughts in any child's mind.

I used to go through the "I am a terrible mother" syndrome whenever I found myself in the position of waving good-bye to my crying child. "She will never forgive me," I would always tell myself. "I should never leave her, even if I never again get a chance to engage in a conversation with someone who is too old to play with his alphabet soup."

But then I talked with a very wise nursery school teacher who told me that a child who is left crying is at least expressing his emotions, while a child who has to deal with his mother sneaking out when he is not looking will end up being afraid to let his parents out of his sight. And, of course, parents do have to get out of their children's sights on occasion. "Let your child know there are things you must do and there are people who will take very good care of her until you get back," this woman advised me. "Don't build on a child's already very real fears of being left alone in the world."

Some parents believe a child experiences less stress when his sugar and caffeine intake is limited. And some teach their children how to relax by picturing pleasant mental scenes. But most parents agree that a child needs to be taught emotional outlets that are socially acceptable.

Don't I know it. When a child is upset and that adrenalin hits, there has to be some form of release. I spent a long time waiting for Becky to turn into one of those sweet, quiet, smiling, perfectly behaved children you see in magazine ads. That was before I realized that those children don't live on my block at all. I finally figured out it is better to talk to your child about some good, healthy ways to relieve stress.

"When you get angry, you can go to your room and cry," I began, "or you can punch your pillows or tear up little pieces of paper." The logical extension of this, I assumed, would be a realization that punching people or tearing them into little pieces is not quite as constructive. I expected, therefore, to end up with a mature child, fully able to handle her negative emotions. But I had forgotten that I was talking to a six-year-old.

Becky turned my advice into a game. She ran to her room, even though she wasn't angry at the time, and began stomping and shouting, with pillow feathers flying and wads of paper crunched up in her mouth. It wouldn't have been nearly as much fun for her if I had just told her she couldn't spend the night with Leah. But I guess it was a step in the right direction. Maybe.

A child needs to learn how to think for himself and take care of himself in order to handle stress. He doesn't need a mother following him around reminding him that brown socks would go better with khaki slacks than blue ones. (After all, are you sure they would at his school?) "I sent my kid off to school yesterday looking like he had said to his clothes, 'I'm going to school; you can come along if you want to,' " one mother sighed, "but he was happy—and he looked like everyone else in class."

In the past, I know I have sometimes been guilty of playing the overpowering mother. So I now try hard to hold down my nagging to the amount that is absolutely necessary to remind me that I am still a mother. I decided to embark on this mission the day I was getting ready to take Becky on a little trip to the mall; and she kept saying to me, over and over, "Are you sure you don't have to go to the bathroom before we leave, Mommy? Just try."

Still, we can take this child-autonomy thing too far. Children do need limits. A young child, for example, is not capable of making intelligent decisions about drugs or alcohol or sex, no matter how much cable TV he watches. Some children aren't even capable of making intelligent decisions about what to take to school for "Show and Tell." (A friend has a son who asked if he could take his new baby sister and leave her on display for a couple of days.) This is why it is so important for us to work with our children where they are, to rehearse situations with them, to give them goals and challenges that will prepare them for life, for those moments when they will walk out the door and feel the tugs: "Do this." "Don't do that." "Come along with us."

"One of the greatest tragedies in today's world," bemoaned a mother of two grown children, "is that when you go up and down the streets, you see so few little children out playing with their parents anymore." When this woman's children were little, she says, the greatest punishment she could give them was to tell them they couldn't go outside and play. This mother is one among many who feel that children are happier and less stress-filled when they are regularly encouraged to get outside and get some exercise.

"When my five kids were small, we had a house that must have measured about twenty-eight by thirty," another mother explained, "so I did everything I could to give them pleasant daily workouts." This woman made a canopied sandbox and taught her children how to build dunes and caves and sand hills. She took them sledding on cardboard boxes—and on nature walks. "We didn't have money for movies and restaurants," she said, "so we went to parks a lot and had picnics or played baseball."

Those kids learned to amuse themselves by tumbling on the dirt and chasing each other until they were worn out or by spinning around in circles until they were too dizzy to stand up. All of the things that make perfect sense in the presence of anyone who can still remember what it feels like to wear training pants. One winter the family even built an igloo.

"Do you remember that igloo we built years ago?" one of those now grown children asked her mother this winter. "Remember how quiet and still it was inside, and how you insisted on crawling through it first so you could watch our expressions as we came through? It was like magic."

Times have changed. Our lives are now structured so that we can't spend every day creating magic with our children. In fact, our days are filled with so much activity—and stress—that most of us cannot even envision a series of afternoons spent exploring our children's worlds with them.

Who's Got the Whole World in His Hands?

"Our world is moving too fast," commented one mother who has a full-time career, "not only for us, but for many of our children." This woman contends that most educational testing is designed for type A personalities (those who work and move quickly and competitively) and that, if those tests were slowed down only a few seconds a question, many type B youngsters (those who work more slowly and relax more easily) would do better in school.

No doubt about it. It is a fast-paced, occasionally frightening world out there with very young children involved in highly competitive sports activities . . . TV sets that only have to be turned on to the nightly news to scare many of our kids to death . . . schools that have to schedule informational programs on sexual abuse in order to insure the safety of the children.

Still, there is hope. There are ways for parents to help prepare their children to face stress in life. One mother decided to reduce stress in her son's life by purchasing an aquarium for him. She had read about research studies claiming that watching fish in aquariums reduces blood pressure and relieves stress.

"The idea worked perfectly," this mother told me. "I think that aquarium lowered the blood pressure of everyone in the family—until it came time to decide who was going to clean it, that is."

We can prepare our children for some of life's stresses, but we can't prepare them for everything. That is why it is so important for children to develop their own inner resources, under their parents' sensitive guidance. It is why we must help our children learn what faith in God is all about.

A friend once told me about a minister who attempted to illustrate the concept of faith during a children's sermon by asking one of the children to fall backward in order to show everyone that God is always there, waiting to catch us. But the minister was standing too far back, and the child ended up sprawled on the floor, crying, kicking, screaming.

"Maybe that's a more realistic picture of faith anyway," my friend said. "Maybe God doesn't promise to take the stresses away, and maybe we don't always feel like He is actually catching us or making the hurt vanish. Maybe we can learn about faith only by taking a few of our own falls."

The stress is never going to disappear. Not for our children and not for us either. Yet, as we and our children learn that God has control of the big issues in life, as we learn to trust Him to bring us through it all triumphantly, we will gradually be able to see purpose in our days. We will gradually be able to see God's hand at work in our lives. And we will finally understand that this is the only thing that was ever truly important all along.

Parting Tips

When your child is learning to handle stress . . .

—Talk with him about his feelings and fears. Prepare him to take his place in the world, and don't turn away when he simply wants to bounce a few of his theories about the obsolescence of your generation off you. Your presence will seem much more acceptable to him when it comes time for him to look for a way to pay his college tuition.

—Most everyone knows that crying helps alleviate stress. A good cry shared with your child probably won't help you solve all your child's problems, but it just might get you through tonight's evening meal without having to contend with a screaming fit over the texture of the creamed corn. And, for many of us, that's not a small thing.

—Don't forget about the importance of good nutrition, ample exercise, peaceful bedtime rituals, and relaxation techniques. Grandmother, in spite of the fact that she never really walked ten miles to school in the snow, could have been right about some things, you know.

—Don't let yourself get too busy to help him with his stress. One definition of too busy: When your child asks you why his dog has to stay at the veterinary hospital overnight, and you answer him by giving him an eight hundred number to call.

—Teach him to meditate, to pray, to be quiet and get in touch with his Creator, who is, after all, the original author of peace.

6

Training Up the Child
Passing Along Values

*"Train up a child in the way he should go, and when he is old he will
not depart from it."*
—Proverbs 22:6, RSV

"No, Becky," I repeated for the fifteenth time, "I am not going
to take you to see that movie. For one thing, it is rated PG-13,
and you're only seven. For another thing, your father has already
said no. And, for a third thing, I don't want to see it myself
because none of the people who are starring in it have even
made it through puberty yet—and, from the looks of most of
them, I doubt if they ever will."

"But Mom," my daughter pleaded, "just because I see something doesn't mean I'm going to do it."

I wonder. Sure, I want to believe that my child is intelligent
enough to do her own thinking. I want to believe she will never
be influenced by the lousy value systems she will invariably encounter in the world. But perhaps that would be unrealistic of
me. Perhaps I am just dreaming.

"Have fun, and be good," I called to my child as she left for
school yesterday morning.

"Mom," she answered, "I'm not sure you can do both at the
same time." Suddenly, I wasn't sure either.

In the last twenty years, the American public has been watching
a lot of premarital sex on TV. We've seen it all around us, in

fact. And, according to an article in *Family Circle* magazine, 85 percent of the parents of college-age youths in 1967 believed premarital sex was morally wrong, whereas, by 1981, 63 percent were condoning it "if two people love each other."

The average eighteen-year-old kid in America has already seen more than one million TV commercials. It would be pretty hard for me to believe that the strange sounding, overpriced items that appear scribbled on my weekly grocery lists have nothing to do with my eight-year-old's contribution to that statistic. If only the ads could show typical American parents telling their children they have to eat sugared cereal because it's so good for them, we'd all be a lot better off. But they don't, because they know, as well as we do, that no self-respecting kid is going to ask his parents for something he thinks is good for him.

Value Development: Back to Basics

Guiding a child's value development is not an easy task. And every parent who takes on that task is bound to find himself, at least on occasion, asking questions like, "How am I ever going to instill any sense of responsibility into someone who can, while sitting all alone in a room, turn over a glass of apple juice with his foot and still say, 'It's not my fault?' " Or, "How am I supposed to teach the meaning of generosity and love to someone who has yet to make it through a meal without saying 'Try to make me!' to his brother?"

Supposedly, our country is beginning to return to more conservative values. Home, hearth, and religion are coming back into style. It is also the generally accepted idea that the family, as the oldest of human institutions, remains the primary channel through which values are passed from one generation to the next—and that much of a child's value system is in place even before he starts school. It would seem, then, that passing along the right values would involve little more than teaching one's children simple moral truths. In fact, we all know it is a lot more complicated than that.

A family's cultural and socioeconomic group must be entered into the mix when you begin talking about a child's value development, as must a number of other factors—like church, school, peer groups, and the media. And, more often than not, a parent eventually finds himself faced with the impossible task of explaining to his children the difference not only between right and wrong but also between sometimes right and sometimes wrong.

How do you tell a child to be honest and kind, but not too honest and kind? How do you avoid having to deal with the child who announces to his family's dinner guests, in total honesty, "Mom bought these yummy steaks because she hopes you'll give Dad a raise this year?" And what can you do except sympathize with the mother who taught her child to be goodhearted and then figured out that her yard had become a foster home for frogs because the child was rescuing all the frogs in neighbors' yards and bringing them home to his own?

"Oh boy," Becky clapped her hands with glee the morning Revis was laid up in bed with a pulled back muscle. "Now I'll have something really neat and different to tell at school sharing time today."

"I am not going to dress my doll before we go to the store!" my friend's little girl screamed, and the child ended up dragging the naked doll along and finding out that supermarkets are filled with mischievous little boys who would rather put their packages of water balloons back on the shelf than miss a chance to tell a cute little girl what they think of her naked doll.

"Embarrassment is not always bad for a child," this little girl's mother insists. "In fact, it can be used to foster an awakening of moral responsibility in the child." But it is only one among the many methods of value instruction.

I think my parents used the humpback/frozen-face method of value instruction with me. For, whenever I did something they disapproved of, no matter what it was, they either told me, "Stand up straight when we talk to you, or your back will grow slump shouldered," or "Don't move your eyes around when we talk to you, or your face will freeze like that."

How to Get Those Values Across

Most parents believe that values are caught, not taught. In actuality, the truth seems to lie somewhere in between. Obviously, the ways Mom and Dad relate to the world (Do they manipulate? Throw fits? Buy people off?) are going to have a drastic effect on their children's value systems. And yet, a child who sees his parents mailing a check to a favorite charity may not grasp the full significance of the act on his own.

We have to let our children see us live our values. We have to refrain from doctoring our income tax returns or getting traffic tickets fixed if we want our children to believe that cheating in school is wrong. But children are not mind readers. We usually have to tell them why we have chosen our values too.

"I've always felt that the worst thing about TV violence," one mother remarked, "is that it is so often portrayed to children as play." This mother went on to talk about the times cartoon characters fall off cliffs or get shot and get right back up, and she said she tries to tell her children how unrealistic this is; but she is not always certain she is getting through. She and her husband are about ready to sell the TV set.

On the other hand, I know another mother and father who actually use TV as a tool to teach their children values. First, they pop some corn and settle down to watch a program together as a family. Then, after the show is over, they talk about it. "What do you remember about the show?" one parent might ask a child. "Which people did you like? Did anyone learn anything in the show? Do you think that's a good lesson for someone to learn?"

True, these parents may not always feel like they have accomplished anything great at the end of such an evening. Once, in fact, they discussed a TV show about an industrious young boy who started his own business and then caught their own son, the following Sunday morning, collecting old church bulletins and trying to sell them to the adult Church School classes. Another time they discussed a program about marriage and later overheard their little girl reenacting the show's wedding ceremony by asking her doll, "Do you, Ken, take Barbie to be your awful wedded wife?" Nevertheless, these parents feel that their efforts will be rewarded in the long run.

I know several parents who insist that it is necessary to involve children, at a very young age, in areas of church and community service. One mother has always let her children help her bake cakes for the bereaved and go along on visits to church shut-ins. "You can't expect your children to believe you care about people if they never see you do anything for anyone," she explained. She is right, of course.

I'll never forget the day Becky's dance class performed at a nursing home. I wasn't at all anxious to take her that day. The weather was terrible, for one thing; and I had seen her class of dancing puppies wiggle their tails so many times. . . . Well, you just don't get too excited about spending an afternoon watching a rear end that you feel like you have spent half of your life cleaning accidents off of.

And yet, I have never been sorry that we trudged through the snow on that occasion. For, after the performance, a very old lady called Becky over and asked if she could touch her face and puppy costume. I could have read my child fifty stories about blind people, and they would never have meant as much to her as the three minutes she spent that day watching that old lady reach out to her—and watching the tears of joy form in those sightless eyes.

Still, all parents have those days when they aren't really in the mood to pass along values, days when they are simply too tired to care. "Mom," Becky giggled when she had just completed her first week of kindergarten, "six boys asked me to marry them today."

"Which one did you choose?" I mumbled, trying to mash the lumps out of a pot of creamed potatoes that were begging me to mash them.

"I told them I'd marry the one who could make the funniest faces," she replied.

"Sounds like as good a way to choose as any I've heard lately."

When I happen upon a day like that, I usually try to say as little as possible. After all, everyone tells me that listening to a child who is in the process of forming his value system, and allowing him to bounce his ideas off you, can be just as important as talking to him.

Of Birds, Bees, and Birth Control

One area of value development that does involve some straight talk is the area of sex education, and all of us have already heard the accepted guidelines. Answer your children's questions when they ask. Don't volunteer more information than they really want. Teach moral responsibility whenever you teach physical facts.

Armed with information like this, I felt ready for anything my daughter might toss my way. From ovulation to Lamaze, I was ready. Of course, what my child actually did toss my way had little to do with either one of these topics—or very much of what would fall in between as far as I could tell.

In the beginning, Becky was convinced that babies are delivered at the post office. Knowing what I know now, I think I would have been very content to leave it at that. But then some kid in kindergarten told Becky that girls have girl babies and boys have boy babies, and she wanted an explanation.

I thought I did a pretty good job of outlining the basics that day. But, when I was done, Becky had one question. She pointed to my stomach and asked, "Do you still have beds and stoves in there so babies can eat and sleep in your stomach?"

The dreaded "How did the sperm get in there?" question wasn't asked until much later. Oddly enough, it was in the middle of a combination business/vacation trip to Cleveland, Ohio. I don't know whether or not there is any significance in the fact that Becky learned about the facts of life in Cleveland. I do know, however, that her response to the whole thing was not surprising. "You're kidding!" she laughed.

My experiences were probably not too unusual. One friend told me she spent a lot of time explaining to her child, as poetically as she could, that God, with the help of Daddy, plants a seed under Mommy's heart; and that seed grows like a flower until a little baby is ready to be born.

"Then when does the mommy vomit the baby up?" was the child's only question.

I always expected the part about the Cesarean section to be the hardest to explain. "Why are other babies born differently than I was?" I could hear Becky asking. "Does that make me different from everyone else?" However, when the time came, my child accepted this part of her birth story very naturally and easily, proving, once again, that parents don't know everything.

Revis and I have never been sorry we spent a lot of time explaining sex to our daughter. We firmly believe that there is nothing like a happy, loving home to set the groundwork for a child's sexual maturation process. We believe, too, that one of the reasons so many of today's teen-agers are sexually promiscuous is that they never see a good, intimate marriage relationship worth striving toward.

A recent TV news show featured a segment on sex education and made the point that giving young people information about sex is no more likely to make them experiment with it than teaching them civics is likely to make them vote. It was a tongue-in-cheek statement, but there is probably a lot of truth in it too. Especially if the young person who is given the sex information is living his life in a Christian atmosphere, in an atmosphere where his parents are convinced that sex is a divinely created gift of God which, when used in the right way, can add a sacred and beautiful dimension to married life.

"Sex was one of God's final, loving steps in creation," said a mother of two, "and if it doesn't remain combined with marital love, it is worth very little." Then she continued, "I once told my teen-age children that people who want a moment of satisfaction with no strings attached might as well eat a lollipop. It's as pleasing to the senses as sex without love, and it doesn't get you pregnant either."

Christian parents have not always been so open about discussing sex with their children. My grandmother never told my mother anything; and we eventually found out that her mother, although she had ten children, always prided herself on the fact that no one (including herself) had ever seen her nude. (She took off one piece of clothing at a time to wash herself.)

I have a friend who was raised on a farm, but was not allowed to see any of the animals give birth. The word *sex* was never mentioned in her home either. "It took me a long time to get over the feeling that sex is a sin so I shouldn't be enjoying it so much," she once told me.

Another family, according to a magazine article I read, had a secret code word for sanitary napkins. They were called marshmallows; and, whenever the word "marshmallow" appeared at the top of the grocery list, everyone knew they needed sanitary napkins. When the word appeared elsewhere on the list, it really meant marshmallows.

We've come a long way all right. Some of us think we have come way too far. And, there is surely not a parent in the world who has never entertained a few questions and doubts along these lines. I once heard Erma Bombeck discussing sex education with a talk show host. She joked ruefully that she had always hoped her kids would get it in the gutters; that way she wouldn't have to teach them! That's an exaggeration, of course, but most of us know what she means. Teaching our children about sex is a daunting proposition. And yet, if we make certain that the values we pass along to our children, even the values surrounding sex, are biblically based, we just might end up reaping the rewards of our efforts after all.

The Unbroken Promise

The Bible tells us that parents who raise their children correctly will end up with children who will not reject the family values. That is a promise. It doesn't say how long it will take the children to come around though. (I can easily visualize it happening to a couple of the little terrors I know on their deathbeds.) And it doesn't say that the children will never rebel.

I know one parent whose child confessed to taking a pack of gum from the corner drugstore fourteen years after the fact, and another whose child went halfway around the world before he decided to adopt his family's moral code. I guess it shouldn't surprise any parent, then, when his five-year-old ignores his pains-takingly taught lessons in selflessness and runs his Tonka truck over the kid who ate his sucker. Or when his six-year-old listens intently to his lectures on modesty and then goes directly to school and moons the entire first grade class. We've all had a few growing pains along the way.

Most experts agree that the times when your children rebel against you are the times when they need your love and support the most. This becomes increasingly important when you remember that a child's basic value system is set between the ages of nine and fourteen—and when you remember that we who are Christian parents are often asking our children to live life differently than some of the people around them.

"I've always told my children what it means to be a Christian," one parent explained. "I've told them that we live differently from non-Christians and that, because of this, we will be asking them not to do some things that their friends at school may be doing." This parent also emphasizes the fact that the guidelines God gives us were devised for our own good, out of perfect love, to make us happy; and he prays, every day, that God will send positive role models into his children's lives. He believes it is a

significant prayer. Especially in light of the fact that there are
so many adults in today's world who clearly never made it past
the "let me have it my way, or I'm going to make you" stage
themselves.

Another parent always reminds his children that he will not
usually be tagging along to see what they are doing, but God
will. This parent encourages his children to talk to God often
during the day, with the understanding that their heavenly Father
will never leave them. "You have to find ways to help your children
see what's truly important and what is trimming in the world,"
he believes, "and most of us spend too much time concentrating
on the wrong things."

As a parent, you probably worry a lot about whether or not
your children are going to "get it right." Will the child be able
to see, in the world around her, that the people who have lousy
morals don't really come out the best in the end? Can an eight-
year-old truly understand? Just the other day I read about some
parents who use home video equipment to watch pornographic
movies, even though their children are running in and out of
the room while the movies are on. "How could such children
not grow up thinking sex is an act in which one person uses
another, possibly even in violent ways?" I began to wonder. "How
can we keep our children from feeling the fallout from people
like that?"

And yet, our children may be learning more about the right
way to live their lives than we think they are. Recently, in fact,
a woman told me that her little girl was running around the
house stepping over Mommy, who was trying to pretend she
didn't have the flu. "You feel bad, Mommy?" the daughter finally
asked, and Mother had to admit that she did. "I'll pray," the
little girl announced, and she bowed her head and asked God
to make her mother all well. At that point, Mommy couldn't
stop the flood of tears she had been holding back all day. But
the child only looked at Mother with a strange expression on
her face and said, "What's wrong, Mommy? I said it right."

We don't always trust the fact that, in many instances, our
children really do know how to "say it right." I sure don't anyway.
Sometimes, I even think it would be nice to be able to open
up Becky's head, pour in the right values, and never let her know
there is any other way. A sort of subliminal *Father Knows Best*

approach. But, down deep, I know how wrong that would be. I know that Becky's values have to be her own—through struggle and doubt, and yes, even pain. The same way values become solidified in the rest of us.

Besides, research among troubled families, even families in which the parents and children are in deep conflict, proves, over and over again, that a child's basic values are very similar to those of his parents. The child may do everything he can to disprove this fact, but the clinical evidence proves otherwise. No matter how hard they try to run away from it, most children do end up openly adopting their parents' values. Eventually.

"Wow," I overheard one young man whisper to another at the beach last summer. "Some people really do have it all."

"I know," the other replied. "Just look at those tans."

At the time, I was glad my child was in the water, out of earshot; but, even then, I knew that she wouldn't always be out of earshot. And I don't suppose I would want to protect her from knowing that those young men have their values misplaced, even if I could. Instead, I guess I will just have to be there for her. And, with a little luck thrown in, I really do think that could be more than enough after all.

Parting Tips

When you are training up your child . . .

—Take advantage of the time when she still wants to be just like Mommy and Daddy. Let her see you acting out some of your best values. She will find out that you once went skinny-dipping in the forbidden pond soon enough.

—Teach her how to say no when she should. It might not be as difficult as it would seem. After all, she's had lots of practice answering you when you've asked her to pick up her toys.

—Don't just give her rules. Give her the reasons behind the rules. It's probably best if you don't call them rules either. There are times when semantics can make all the difference in the world.

—Apologize to her whenever you are wrong. If I ever am, I'm sure going to.

—Never preach. Only the minister in his pulpit on Sunday morning can get away with that. And, even then, it doesn't always work.

7

Your Child and God

Religious Education

"To have knowledge, you must first have reverence for the Lord."
—Proverbs 1:7, TEV

"It is extremely difficult to be religious in today's world," a minister once told me, "for you must either be a fanatic or a saint—and I don't know too many saints."

Those words hit me the hardest when I think about raising a child to be a Christian in the midst of this crazy, mixed-up world. For, I see so many young people around me today who are not being taught anything about God—young people who think that redemption has something to do with supermarket coupons and that Deuteronomy would be a great name for a rock group.

"But what about the Bible?" you ask them.

"We saw the movie, but we didn't read the book."

Is it possible to effectively introduce our children to their heavenly Father in such an environment? Most Christian parents believe that it is, as long as we know our offspring well enough to work with them on their own level.

Young Enough to Know Better

A five-year-old child who has learned trust from her parents is ready for a simple dependence upon God. She is beginning to understand the Bible stories her parents read to her, although she may not always appear to be doing so. (One mother told me about her five-year-old forgetting his lines during the church Christmas pageant and introducing the wise men with the words, "Well, here come the three wise guys with bottles of Avon to give to the baby Jesus.")

The five-year-old responds well to role play, especially if you can convince him that he is going to be the star. He might have to have a lot of terms explained to him though. The little boy who had never visited a Baptist church until the Sunday he visited ours certainly did. The child simply could not understand why we had a "bathtub" in our church, but the friend who had brought him quickly set him straight. "That's not a bathtub," he whispered. "It's a bathtismal."

Then there is the issue of conscience. Many people agree that a child's conscience begins to show some development around age three. Of course, you would probably never be able to guess that from looking at a typical preschool child, particularly when he has his sister in a hammer lock. But I do remember one day when Becky was about five and had seen a television documentary about poor people. She was trying to call the number on the TV screen and offer them her new cassette tape of *Cinderella*.

"I just wanted to help," Becky later disclosed. "I felt sad clear down in my heart." I didn't have the heart to tell my child that poor people don't have cassette tape players—or that listening to the story of Cinderella probably wouldn't cheer them up anyway.

Some five-year-olds experience moments of awe during worship services, I am told. Surely, those moments must be of the fleeting variety, since most kids that age sit in church with friends who like to take turns drawing Big Bird on each others' backs. But if the moments do exist at all, I suppose that must mean something.

I do know that there are many ways to teach a five-year-old about God. You can appeal to his desire to collect things, for instance, and take him on a Bible study nature walk. Or, you can point out that his simple household chores are important because God's Word teaches us to be kind and helpful.

This is also the perfect age to concentrate on the child's growing prayer life and to encourage him to talk to God in his own personal way. "Dear Lord," Becky began her prayer one evening when she hadn't taken a nap at kindergarten, "please watch over me at the party tonight, even if I am mean."

Prayer before meals is considered passé in many of today's Christian homes. Maybe because the people in those homes have become so busy that family meals themselves are now passé. At any rate, it would be a great activity to reinstate. Not because food can't digest unless it is celebrated with the words "God is great; God is good," but because the children in a Christian home need to hear their parents pray and because those children need to be given the opportunity to talk comfortably with God in their own languages.

"When my kids were little, they used to fight about who would get to say grace," one mother sighed, "but when they got older, they fought about who was going to have to say it." Sounds typical. The younger they are the easier it seems to be for them. A case in point: One of Becky's first table graces, spoken at age three and duly recorded in her baby book by her doting mother was as follows. "Dear Ga, tank you for today. Tank you for Mrs. Jones' new funny looking baby. You and Jesus live in heaven. We live in Ohio state. We eat real food. Cows give milk. Amen." It was a crucial beginning.

By the time Becky was six, she was telling God jokes at the end of each of her prayers—and asking me if I thought she was making Him laugh. Judging from most of the prayers God has to listen to (the type I've heard, anyway), I was able to tell her, in total honesty, "Yes, Becky, I think that is probably the best laugh God has had all day."

The Early Grade-School Child and Spiritual Things

The six-year-old, secure in her parents' love, has already learned a lot about trust. Your job is to find ways to encourage her to place more and more of that trust in God. A child's faith is still simple at this point, but we must never underestimate its power. I found this out when Becky decided to pray for sunshine for her sixth birthday. (I was the one who should have been praying, since I was really the one who was hosting the lawn party for twenty-five of my child's sticky-fingered little friends.)

Like any good, logical Christian parent, I tried to explain to my child that, since it had rained for twelve straight Sundays, she shouldn't be disappointed if God chose not to grant her prayer. (What could I say? Maybe some Cub Scout den mother somewhere was praying for a camping trip to be rained out.) My daughter looked at me as if I were crazy, as if she knew something I didn't. Probably because she did.

The movies of Becky's sixth birthday party, held on a Sunday afternoon, attest to the fact that she had to wear sunglasses to open her presents.

These are the years when the child is growing fast, and they are the years when abstract thinking begins. The child becomes more aware of other people's feelings and more intrigued by the difference between right and wrong. Maybe not intrigued enough to keep him from organizing shaving cream fights at church camp, but at least it's a step in the right direction. Soon, a clearer concept of sin and forgiveness will begin to emerge in him.

This is the time when many churches give Bibles to their children. It is also the time for the parents to help those children learn how to use those Bibles. And it is the time for children to begin to sense that there is a deeper meaning behind many of the Bible stories they have heard.

Memory verse recitation never went over very well in our house. (Was it fun when I was a kid, or did it just give me an excuse to stand next to my Sunday School heartthrob—whose last name began with the same letter as mine?) Becky has always enjoyed Bible story crossword puzzles and mazes though, and I have often used them to nurture the development of her maturing image of God.

"God probably has black curly hair, a mustache, an orange hat with red stripes, and sandals," my daughter told me when she was five.

"You can't see God," she told me when she was seven, "but He sent us Jesus in the form of a human being, and people sure saw Him."

When you are teaching children in early grade school about God, it helps to remember that they love to cut, paste, paint, and work with rocks or leaves. Thus, you can make Bible collages with them, you can encourage them to build a miniature Bible city, or you can let them help you plant a tree in the yard as you talk to them about the parable of the sower. Children of this age might even feel good about taking part in a regular family devotion time—if you are careful to tread very softly.

Family devotions went the way of table grace a long time ago in many Christian homes. Maybe this is because we got too busy. Or maybe it is because we got too tired of our children asking to be excused to go to the bathroom in the middle of family prayers or punching their siblings and giggling when they were told about the "king who comes riding on an ass." A friend of mine once tried conducting family worship experiences centered around Old Testament Hebrew customs. His children were three, five, and seven at the time. He should have waited a few years.

"And what do you know about the Jewish people?" the father inquired with great enthusiasm the first night of the study.

"There's one kid in kindergarten who's Jewish," the five-year-old replied.

"We don't have any Jewish kids in our class," the seven-year-old added, "but we have one kid whose dad works at a pizza parlor."

"What does that have to do with anything?" the father asked impatiently.

"His name is Jeremy," the child answered, as if that explained the whole thing. Then the other children started laughing hysterically because, the father later found out, the children at school thought Jeremy was a funny name and had, therefore, nicknamed the boy "Germy."

A couple of nights later, the family worship time seemed to be going better. Until the five-year-old asked a question about the Jewish child in her class. "Is Kenny a reformed Jew or an orthodontist Jew?" was the question. Giggles began to permeate the air.

"Oh," the young girl continued, in an embarrassed tone of voice, "that's right. An orthodontist is an eye doctor, isn't it?"

After that, the other children became uncontrollable, and their poor father decided that, if it was going to be left up to him, his children would simply have to grow up without knowing anything about Hebrew history.

So many times, family devotions turn into fiascoes—perhaps because children are so used to being entertained with fantastic special effects these days, and most parents don't have the equip-

ment or the "talent" to film music videos to accompany their
Bible lessons. Or perhaps it has always been difficult to get little
children to enjoy sitting still and reading the Bible.

Many people tell me they made the mistake of spending their
devotion time plowing headlong through scriptures like "And
Aram begat Aminadab" with their children until even the parents
began taking turns going to sleep. A number of these people
eventually began using family-centered devotional guides during
their worship experiences. Others found it to be simply impossible
to fit in a structured family worship experience every day; and,
instead, switched to once a week family gatherings and nightly
bedtime prayer.

Some families keep prayer journals. They note in these the
dates of family prayer requests and the dates when those requests
are answered. These families talk about how meaningful it is to
go back and read their journals—and to discover that many of
their prayers were answered five, ten, or fifteen years down the
road. When the time was truly right.

Most parents I know tell me they encourage their children's
input in making decisions about family worship, and they also
tell me that life changes so quickly that they have to make changes
in their formats pretty often.

How to Reach Today's Child

Sometimes I think our methods of religious education in the
home are not intentional enough. After all, God's instruction to
us in the Scriptures is built around our responsibility to keep
His commandments in our hearts and repeat them to our children.
He even told the Hebrew people to bind those commandments
as a sign on the hand, wear them as a phylactery on the forehead,
and write them on the doorposts of houses. Obviously, God wants
us to make sure that our faith permeates our homes in many
intentional ways. He doesn't want us to take the chance that
our children will catch faith in Him by osmosis.

A child knows what is truly important to his parents. Thus,
we have the five-year-old boy playing "I have to work late" so
he can be just like Daddy. And we have the seven-year-old girl
who says she doesn't know how much her mom weighs because
she is always on a diet, but the child plans on being a great

mommy when she grows up because she already knows how to "go on a diet and lose a few pounds."[2] One of the most effective ways to emphasize the importance of the Christian faith to one's children is through the use of ritual and tradition—repetition, over and over, until one's total being is saturated with the activity.

"My children acted like they could care less about many of our religious traditions when they were growing up," reported a mother of five, "but the year I tried to vary the Christmas dinner menu of turkey, ham, and oysters, they really let me have it." Then she added, "It all takes with your kids. Don't you ever believe it doesn't."

"Wherever I am at 6:00 P.M., my stomach turns over," smiled a young college coed, "because six o'clock was the cast-in-stone traditional dinner hour in my home."

Good, meaningful Christian traditions can often be built around holidays, and many parents insist that there are lots of creative family worship ideas published around the times of Advent and Lent. (It seems that anything with candles is great to use with little children.) Some families rent video equipment and shoot real home movies of their Christmas family worship celebrations. Other family rituals include taking turns, at Thanksgiving dinner, enumerating the blessings for which they are thankful.

Rituals are extremely important. And yet, we must never overlook the obvious. For, one of the best ways to share the Christian faith with our children still remains taking them to church with us.

Within the Hallowed Walls

There is no doubt about it. Most early grade-school children are capable of getting something out of a church worship experience. That's the good news. The bad news is that they can't sit still long enough to do so—which is probably why so many churches provide special programs for young children during Sunday morning worship experiences.

There are parents who get disturbed by this. They feel their children have begun to mature in the Christian faith and that those children shouldn't be marched out of church right before the sermon, as if it were X-rated or something. They fear that

their children will grow up knowing little about their church beyond the quality of its punch and cookies.

Personally, I have never felt any of this is really worth getting
upset about. I think it is more important to make sure your child
is getting quality Christian training somewhere in the church and
good Christian nurture at home. I must admit, however, that
my opinion has probably been influenced by my cousin's young
son, who once stood up on a pew in the middle of a Sunday
morning sermon, pretended he was He-Man, and, waving a toy
sword, started yelling at the top of his lungs, "I am the power."

On the other hand though, I do think it is critically important
that the whole family be actively involved in the church together.
I may not understand everything about the scriptural idea that
the father should be the priest in the home; but I do know that,
at the very least, it means that a Christian father who is living
up to his responsibilities doesn't stay home in bed on Sunday
morning while his family trudges off to church. Study after study
has proven me correct. For, the children who stick with church
the longest are invariably the ones who were accompanied there
by dear old Dad.

Of course, we may not always get something fantastic out of
every worship service we attend. So, we shouldn't tell our children
that they will. But, then again, maybe we should. . . . I spent
lots of Sunday mornings scribbling my week's dinner menus on
church bulletins before it finally dawned on me that my Church
School teacher never failed to gain some great spiritual truth
from every one of those worship services. Eventually, I got up
the nerve to ask him why.

"Before I go into any worship experience," he told me, "I always
pause and ask God to speak to me in some way through it."
And there it was. I was looking at life through earth-bound eyes—
seeing the pastor's mismatched suit and tie or the unbelievable
girth of the soprano, whose tumultuous sound was almost as
big as her hips. But my Church School teacher was seeing beyond
all that because he was looking at life through spiritual eyes;
he was using his time to converse with God Himself.

A child deserves to be taken to a good, solid, friendly church.
He deserves to be in the midst of a people of God who are
grappling with life issues, and loving each other all the while.
He needs to be in a church made up of people who have strong
convictions, but who are willing to allow each individual to find

his own way. And yet, no church is perfect; and what a child needs most of all are Christian parents who are always looking for ways to reveal God's saving power to him.

Beyond the Hallowed Walls

As parents we bring to our children who and what we are in terms of our own spiritual pilgrimages. We bring to them the statement that everything we do is, in fact, a Christian act because we are Christians. Many of the people I know say they never thought much about Christianity when they were growing up because it wasn't real enough to their parents. How did they know? Few people are as perceptive as little children. Sometimes, in fact, children even notice what goes on around them much more often than we wish they would.

A friend once told me a story about her nephew's growing-up years, and about the day he went on his first train ride to visit his grandmother. "This grandmother was everything a grandmother should be," the woman explained, "blue hair, sweet little hats—a tiny, dainty, prim little lady with frou-frous around her neck." On the way home from the visit, Grandmother and Grandson were sitting together on the train, right next to a woman who was very discreetly nursing her baby.

"Grandma," the boy began screaming, "that baby's eating his mamma." For the rest of the train ride, the grandmother was unable to reason with the child, or to quiet him down. By the time the two arrived at their destination, Grandmother was so perturbed that she made the boy walk behind her so no one would know they were together.

Children are perceptive. They are aware, and this isn't necessarily bad. Especially when you consider the fact that a child cannot just adopt his parents' faith. He has to go out and find his own, and this generally takes quite a bit of discernment and insight.

By the time a child is old enough to begin struggling with the issues of personal faith, he is too old for force tactics to do any good. (I'm not sure I have ever been able to accomplish anything by force with my children. In fact, I still remember my determination to get Becky to eat strained peas. As far as I know, that bowl of peas could still be sitting on the kitchen table of our first apartment.)

Yet, one significant fact remains in our favor—the fact that each of our children has an emptiness inside that can only be filled by God. Children were made that way. They may do a lot of searching before they understand it, but they were made that way. Then there is also the fact that God speaks to our children, even when they are very young.

"Becky, would you please put Jesus in the manger box?" I said to my daughter when she was about five years old and we were putting away the Christmas decorations.

"Okay, Mommy," she bubbled, "but the real Jesus can't go in a box because He lives inside me."

"Did I tell her that?" I asked myself, amazed. I was sure I must have, but when a child responds to your greatest pronouncements with statements like, "Tommy named his pet hamster Raisin Bran because that's his favorite cereal," I guess you just have trouble believing she will retain any of it.

Revis and I have always felt it very crucial to teach our children that Christianity is a growth process—not something you profess and then sit there like a packet of hot chocolate, waiting for the miraculous waters to make you instantly good. But grace is a hard concept for any child to grasp.

"If I don't get to heaven by being bad or good, then why do I have to share my candy bar with Todd?" Becky asked me one day. It was a good question. I know a lot of adults who still think like that.

Oh well, I never said I could get through all of this with great ease, with no mistakes, and with my sanity completely intact. After all, we parents only *try* to love our children perfectly. God is the one who accomplishes it.

Parting Tips

When you are introducing your child to Jesus . . .

—Discuss his Church School lesson with him—and treat yourself to a good little refresher course in Bible knowledge at the same time.

—Be careful what you tell him about God. He just might believe you.

—Emphasize the yeses of your religion instead of the noes. And promise yourself always to make positive statements about your minister and church leaders in your home, even when the sermon is on tithing.

—Stay alert. A friend once told me that 9:30 A.M. was the hour for misbehavior in his home when he was growing up because the children knew that this was the hour when their mother would be "in prayer."

—Give yourself little pop quizzes along the way. Keep asking yourself, "What kind of people am I raising in my home?" And, "Are these the people God created them to be?"

8

There Really Was a Gorilla in My Room, Mommy

Imagination and Creativity

"The Lord by wisdom founded the earth; by understanding he established the heavens."

—Proverbs 3:19, RSV

There is no doubt about it. Preschool children are extremely creative little beings. Strange, maybe. Rambunctious, perhaps. But definitely creative.

"I think the tooth fairy has blonde curly hair and a long blue dress," Becky remarked when she was about to enter kindergarten. "I think she has skinny knees, too, and wings; and she probably checks kids' mouths while they are sleeping to make sure it's really their teeth and not stolen ones."

I have a friend whose little boy grew up with an imaginary pal named Jimmy Juggler. Each night at dinner, a place had to be set at the table for Jimmy. Then, one night, the child's father, tired from a long day at work and afraid that his son's imagination was getting out of hand, stood up from the table, grabbed Jimmy Juggler by the collar, and proceeded to throw this imaginary person out the door. The child cried so desperately that his father finally had to go outside and invite Jimmy back into the house.

Most of us parents can easily identify with experiences like these, watching our children leave their special marks on each new day . . . deciding that they are surely bright enough to change the world singlehandedly . . . worrying that they might be spending too much time in fairy-tale worlds. How do you achieve that magic balance between order and creativity? How do you stimulate a child's imagination and channel his creativity into positive expression without losing your own sanity?

Creativity is defined as self-expression, originality, imagination. It is the distinctive flair that a person brings to his work, his hobbies, his relationships, indeed most everything in his life. You don't have to be an artist or a songwriter to be creative. You can use your creativity to arrange fresh flowers on the dinner table or to devise a new way to persuade a business client to accept your proposal or to write a meaningful thank-you note. Your children will notice all of this, too, and they might even learn something from it.

As parents we can help our children expand their creative abilities. Creativity is believed to have little to do with a person's IQ. Instead, it is something a human being can develop. And yet, it is something that many people, for one reason or another, never do develop. In fact, the opposite seems to be true—they tend to lose what they once had.

There is a Charles Schulz cartoon showing Snoopy sitting on a bicycle; the caption reads, "Life is like a ten-speed bicycle. Most of us have gears we never use." A speaker at a recent Christian youth convention said it another way. "Only 2 percent of today's adults are using their God-given creativity," she explained, "and, while 90 percent of all five-year-olds are highly creative people, only 20 percent of seven-year-olds would fall into that category."

Obviously, a part of the problem here is that a school-age child is taught to follow instructions, to sit in a row, to write the same words in the reading workbook as the child at the next desk. Thus, we have the grade-school open houses with the walls full of precisely matching Halloween pumpkins that look so boring you wonder why no one thought of mixing them all up together and making a pie. Writer Fredelle Maynard, writing for *Woman's Day* magazine, put it this way: "The average fourth grade, in short, is full of children who have learned to do approved things in conventional ways."

Of course, this is not all bad. Particularly for the school teacher who doesn't want to end up in the psychiatric ward of the nearest hospital. For there are some children who would drive their teachers crazy very quickly if they were allowed to engage in their own personal brands of creative activity at school. I know one child, for example, whose idea of creativity is finding new ways to throw food—and several others who are not interested in creating anything unless it involves sending at least one adult to bed with a cold compress on his head.

I'll never forget an evening during Christmas break two years ago. Revis, Becky, and I had decided to get dressed up and spend the perfect family evening together at some overpriced restaurant. I guess it must have slipped my mind that on a seven-year-old's list of fun things to do, dining out in style ranks about two points below going to a tea party with her mother.

The evening got off to a good start, but soon Becky began getting "creative." First, she told a funny story about her father being an impostor daddy dressed up to look like her real daddy, with a drawn-on mustache and a piece of white paper pasted on his head to look like her real daddy's bald spot. At that point, the whole thing was mildly amusing. (At least to me. I'm not the one with the bald spot.) But, before long, Becky's seven-year-old powers of imagination began to take over; and she soon had herself scared to death that her story might be true. Nothing we could say would convince her otherwise. (Revis even got desperate enough to let her walk over and touch his bald spot.)

Eventually, things got so bad that Becky was sobbing, "Mommy told me she would bring my real daddy to the restaurant. I'm afraid Mommy doesn't even know who my real daddy is." Needless to say, the evening became pretty embarrassing after that; and I could see that I was either going to have to cut the evening short or risk assuming the role of a very tainted woman.

There are times in every parent's life when he simply cannot allow his child's creativity to run rampant. There are more times, however, when the parent must do everything possible to encourage that child to be creative.

In Search of the Building Blocks

Listening to a young child's questions and stories is one of the most important, and often most difficult, tasks of being a parent. "Did the pilgrims wear pajamas, Mommy?" Becky once asked me. "And how can God be everywhere at once? And do ministers learn to sit on the potty when they are three?" Most children's questions are like that. Complete surprises, seldom divided into subject matter, and totally unanswerable to anyone's satisfaction. Such questions are often asked at the wrong times, too. I found that out the day I decided it would be cute to take my little daughter to a fashion show in Cleveland, Ohio. That was the day Becky inquired, right in the middle of the luncheon, in a very loud voice, "How do the daddies get the seeds into the mommies?"

Many of my friends have had similar experiences with their children's questions and stories. Take Julia, for instance. She had spent the entire spring season teaching her son, Billy, the story of the Resurrection; and she had done her job well. So well, in fact, that Billy was asked to give his rendition of "The True Story of Easter Sunday" during his church's Easter play.

When it came time for the program, Julia was ready to play the role of proud parent—and Billy was determined not to let her down. He started telling the story of the Crucifixion, cops and robbers style, with such enthusiasm that the entire congregation was hanging on every word. So was his mother, until Billy's Church School teacher asked him to tell everyone who rolled away the stone.

"The Easter Bunny did," Billy replied, with the proudest grin ever to grace the mouth of a five-year-old.

No matter how much energy it takes, the parent who wants to help his child develop creativity has to spend a lot of time listening to questions and stories that no one else over the age of six could be paid to listen to. He also has to remember that a young child is going to believe just about everything his parents tell him. My aunt and uncle learned that particular lesson the hard way the year my little cousin Charles became very attached to his pet rabbit.

"I think Chatsworth is just about ready to be cooked and eaten now," Charles' father told him one day, with a chuckle in his voice. But Charles wasn't chuckling—and neither was Chatsworth Rabbit. Later that day, in fact, Charles ended up riding home to his distraught parents in a police car, a frightened little boy with wet pants who had with him Chatsworth Rabbit and a small suitcase into which he had tucked a pair of shorts.

"I think the police were very glad to get rid of my son that day," his mother smiled, "and his father and I were very careful never to mention fried rabbit in the house again."

This is how most of us parents learn—by experience, as we begin to work with our children and find ways to teach them and nurture them and encourage them.

Igniting the Spark of Creativity

"If you want your children to be creative," explains pastoral counselor Kenneth Story, "you have to affirm the things they do that have worth." According to Dr. Story, there are a million ways to do this—a touch, a smile, a wink, a kind word. "Most parents attack what their children do wrong much more often than they affirm what their children do right," says Dr. Story. "In fact, just about every family I work with has fallen into this trap."

I suspect this means that I am going to have to look for the perfect thread to praise in a lot more potholders before I am done raising my daughter. It probably means I am going to have to laugh at a lot more of her unmistakably original jokes, too. Lately, I think I must have begun shirking that part of my parental responsibility because I've noticed that Becky has started prefacing her punch lines with the words, "Now here comes the funny part, Mom." Evidently, I haven't been laughing in the right places.

"But how am I supposed to react?" a friend sighed when I told her what I had learned about the importance of affirming your children's work. "Jeffrey doesn't think anything is a true masterpiece unless it's made out of some form of dirt, and I have trouble managing a sincere smile when my child's works of art leave trails throughout my house."

"Maybe a not-so-sincere smile would do in that case," I shrugged. "Or you might try telling yourself he will probably grow up to be a famous archaeologist."

"Maybe," she replied. "Either that or a mud wrestler."

Of course, there is more to creativity than having one's work affirmed. Creative people have also learned how to be flexible. They have been taught not only how to cope with a changing world, but how to joyfully open themselves up to it.

"Any phone messages?" I asked Becky one day when I had left her at home and gone to the market.

"Yes, Mommy," she answered nonchalantly, "a computer called."

Every day I am reminded of the fact that my daughter is growing up in a rapidly changing world. She doesn't even believe me anymore when I tell her there actually was real life before pocket calculators and jogging shoes.

"I'm really out of it, I guess," one mother recently told me. She had spent the previous day taking her little girl shopping for school clothes. I could tell. We all have "that look" when we've just blown a week's grocery money on a "must-have" piece of kid's clothing that, left alone, we wouldn't have spent ten cents on at a yard sale.

"I know what you mean," I assured her. "I just read about a woman who thought Ewok was something you cook Chinese food in, and I quickly identified with her, even though I've seen the *Star Wars* movies.

"I'll never take my child to visit an Amish village again," another friend commented, "educational experience or not." Her child had spent the day pointing to people and squealing, "Look, Mom. They're from *Little House on the Prairie!*"

It's enough to make you wonder how you are ever going to understand today's world well enough to open it up to your children. And yet, there is another option. We can always work with our children to open up our individual worlds to each other. We can listen to them, really listen, when they talk about their hopes and dreams. And we can share our own hopes and dreams with them.

Teaching Your Child How to Dream

The creative people in our world are the people who have been exposed to life. They are not generally the kind of people who sit around the house a lot. Instead, they are the kind of people who love to see things, do things, explore.

One parent learned a lesson in creativity the day she hid behind the bushes and followed her son home from elementary school. She was concerned because it always took him an hour longer than anyone else to get home. What she saw that day is a sight she will never forget.

"At every crack in the sidewalk, he would stop and watch the little ants," this mother observed. "Then he would move on to a tiny leaf or flower, which he would carefully pick up and scrutinize and then place back exactly where it had been." Watching her son explore his world like that, this woman began to remember what it felt like to be a kid. Until then, she had almost lost the wonder. "After that, I never said a word to my son about being late from school," she explained, "because he was seeing things that the rest of us hurry right by."

The creative people in our world are also the ones who were taught to appreciate great art, literature, drama, and music at an early age. Of course, it never hurts to use a little common sense during this exposure process. For, there are those children who simply cannot seem to remember that the Metropolitan Opera is not a sing-along. Such a child is probably better off listening to classical records at home for a while.

One night I took Becky and a five-year-old houseguest to a local musical. I thought it would be good for them, so I ignored their assurances that they would rather stay home with a baby-sitter and pretend to be giraffes. *No comparison,* I thought. *What could they possibly get out of playing giraffe, except maybe a strained neck?* So, I toted them along.

"My, my, your children are behaving nicely," an elderly woman smiled, patting their heads. And she was right. They were behaving nicely. But they had been in the theater only three minutes at the time. "You're fortunate to have a mother who will take you little children out like this," the woman continued, obviously pressing her luck. "Most little children don't get to go to things like this."

She had gone too far. Soon, the little boy was shouting, "But we didn't want to come," and Becky was mumbling something about the lucky kids who get to stay home and be giraffes. The elderly woman was clearly too far removed from life with children (or giraffes) to understand any of this, so she quickly moved on, leaving me to deal with two unruly children who were, by that time, insisting that they had to go to the bathroom—"bad!"

There are many ways you can help foster creativity in your children, even on those days when they are too rowdy to be taken out of the house. You can encourage them to make up songs and create works of art, for example. Or you can show them how to write their ideas and feelings in their own personal journals.

"We didn't have much money when the kids were growing up," my friend Raetta once told me, "so we couldn't afford a lot of mechanical type things." Raetta insists that she is glad about that today. For, although she believes mechanical toys can help further a child's technical abilities, she doesn't think they do anything for the imagination.

Raetta's children often had to rely on the old cake pan with the sliding lid for indoor entertainment. Into the pan, they would put their crayons, scissors, paper, puzzles cut from old magazines, and always a little ledger to write in. "Once we went on vacation, all the way from the Midwest to Florida," Raetta explained, "with six kids, ages three to twelve, and that old cake pan." Then she added, with a smile, "If I hadn't been little more than a kid myself, I might have known enough to exhibit some sensible apprehension about the whole thing."

The children in this family are grown now, but their mother still has that old cake pan ("to look at on those days when I feel kind of down"). Recently, she dug out the ledger and discovered that her oldest son had recorded the date when he saw his first Spanish moss. "It looks like a tree that is letting it all hang out," the entry reads.

You don't have to have a lot of money to raise creative children. In fact, with just a little imagination, you can probably come up with some simple creative games that are better than money could ever buy. I tried to do this the day Becky was in bed with the flu and was refusing to drink her liquids. That was when I invented the liquid elf. Every time a glass was empty and the child's eyes were closed, the liquid elf would come and replace the glass with something new to drink. The idea worked so well that I almost ran out of juices.

Eventually, Becky decided to start writing notes to the liquid elf. The elf then had to answer the notes, and the game became a bit more complicated than I had planned. ("Do you think the elf can write poems and make up songs, Mommy?") Still, I figured, "What the heck. Sick kids never let you get anything done anyway. And this might turn out to be at least as much fun as trying to get medicine down a person who has never voluntarily let anything that wasn't coated in chocolate enter her mouth." Of course, my husband thought I was crazy, hopping around the house like that. But I challenged him to spend the day with a sick, cranky kid and then tell me he wouldn't rather be an elf. The subject was quickly dropped.

Exploring God's Unfinished World

We can teach our children a lot about God when we are encouraging them to be creative. For, God was the one who created the world in the first place, the one who chose to leave that world unfinished, waiting for us to build the bridges and write the music and sculpt the masterpieces. "God did this on purpose," I assured Becky one day, "because He made you with the intelligence and ability to do these things." Granted, her creativity was being used to create a mess on the living room floor at the time, but I've always felt that it can't hurt to toss out a gem of wisdom here and there among the toys.

I know one woman who made sure that her children became aware of God's world by devising a game called "thing finding." She would allow her two children to go down opposite sides of the block and spend thirty minutes finding "things" to bring home and examine. When all of the treasures were spread out on the table, the children would compare their finds. Then, they would examine each thing individually, sometimes with a magnifying glass, so that they could see the softness of a butterfly wing or the intricate detail of a tiny stem.

"I told them that God is in everything," this mother remembers, "and, sure enough, we did find Him in each of our things." This woman's son is now a celebrated anatomy professor who lectures in Germany and her daughter is involved in many creative endeavors as a wife, mother, and artist. "They are sophisticated people today," their mother told me, "but they never lost that sense of wonder and awareness."

Another way to inspire spiritual creativity in a child is to work in some topnotch Christian literature among that cartoon caravan of bedtime stories. Thus, Revis was reading *The Chronicles of Narnia* to Becky before she could even pronounce its title. Mostly, I think he just wanted an excuse to re-read the books himself, but I could be wrong. At least I know that Becky started loving the stories very early in life. She even asked some pretty sensitive questions about great authors one day.

"Can anyone write really good books for children and really good books for adults, too?" was one of those questions.

"Most people can do one much better than the other," I explained, "but you know C. S. Lewis wrote *The Chronicles of*

Narnia; and he also wrote some wonderful books for adults, so he was one writer who could do both."

"Wow," my daughter replied. "He sounds like he could do anything." Then, after much thought, she added, "Could he do a back flip, too?"

Leave it to a child to cut right through to the back flips. And yet, most of our efforts to encourage creativity in our children are probably doing a lot more good than we think they are. For, once we have ignited the spark, our children, when they are ready, will be prepared to go out and look more closely at their divinely created world. They will also be prepared to search, carefully and imaginatively, for ways that they, as the pearls of God's creation, can best give themselves to that world.

Parting Tips

When you are looking for ways to foster creativity in your child . . .

—Introduce her to the public library when she is very young. Let her have her own library card. But don't expect her to start out choosing a Shakespearean volume over *Tommy Turtle Looks for His Shell*. After all, are you even sure that *you* would voluntarily choose a Shakespearean volume over *Tommy Turtle Looks for His Shell?*

—Teach her about your hobbies—and let her teach you about hers. Maybe collecting dead ants is not your first choice among things to do for a fun afternoon, but it could be worse. At least she's not yet collecting phone numbers of members of the opposite sex.

—Never discourage her sensitivity and her ability to feel things deeply. This is important whether your child is a boy or a girl. None of today's self-respecting little girls are going to grow up and marry a man who can't feel strongly enough about his children to hold his own in a parent-teacher conference anyway.

—Teach her to enjoy being alone. You may have to compete with a tape player and fifty stereo records, but never give up.

—Explore God's creation with her. And let her see the beauty of the world through the eyes of someone who has a personal relationship with its maker.

9

Laughing All the Way to the Fifth Knothole Game of the Week

Humor in the Home

"A clever man has the wit to find the right way . . ."
—Proverbs 14:8, NEB

Many of the experiences involved in raising children are very humorous. Unfortunately though, most of it doesn't seem funny until you are too old to care. Still, family life should be a lot more fun than it often is.

In Quest of Real Life

Recently, I looked up the definition of the word *vibrant* in the dictionary. I found out it means "pulsating with life, vigor, or activity; open and responsive to environment, events, other people." That's what the Christian should be like, I reasoned. That's what the Christian's family life should be all about.

"I wasn't feeling very vibrant the night my son won a goldfish at the school carnival," one mother told me, "but I guess I should have been more understanding of his right to have his own kind of fun." This mother had made her son promise not to play any of the games with live prizes, but the boy had been such a helpful member of the carnival clean-up committee that one of the teachers (clearly out to get revenge for the hamster she had received from her class as a Christmas present the year before) had given him a leftover goldfish in appreciation.

"As a result," the boy's mother explained, "I had to invest in an aquarium ('You wouldn't make someone you love sleep in a jar, would you, Mommy?'), lots of fish food (table scraps didn't go over too well), and a mate (I guess I'm a sentimental romantic at heart)." By the time all of this had been done, the original goldfish had died. Twenty years down the road, the whole experience is going to seem hysterical.

We need to learn to enjoy our children more. Maybe not when the dog has forgotten to scratch on the door and the soup is boiling over on the stove and everyone in the house is fighting to watch favorite TV shows—but we ought to enjoy our children sometimes. Perhaps even most of the time.

The ability to make every day count is a by-product of one's relationship with God. For, the closer we get to our heavenly Father, the more direction we will have for our lives and the better understanding we will have of our goals and priorities. But there is more to it than even that. The Christian who wants to live every day of his life must also plan his days to that end.

I have one friend who became determined, a short time ago, to plan more fun into her daily schedule—in spite of the fact that she has three kids who equate having a good time with pretending to be carsick whenever she is driving the neighborhood carpool.

These days, this woman is always on the lookout for ways to build her own brand of fun into her daily schedule. Most of her ideas have been surprisingly well received by the other members of her family, too. Occasionally, she gets ideas from magazine articles, like the one she read that suggested a celebration of winter being half over. She decorated the house with flowers, served a picnic dinner, and showed old movies of summer vacations.

My friend doesn't get this elaborate every night. Some days she simply doesn't have the energy. Some days she has spent too many hours playing school room mother, passing out Dixie Cups to kids whose mouths are already permanently stained with grape juice. But she does manage to spend a lot of her spare time making some pretty interesting memories, often by luxuriating in the "simple" things of life—a gorgeous sunrise or sunset, or a cherished old record she had almost forgotten about.

I have another friend who has always been really good at having fun with her kids. "You wanted children, didn't you?" she often says to people. "Then play with them. Have fun with them."

It sounds so simple coming from her. Maybe she has never had a kid whose idea of cleaning up his own messes is yelling, "Mom, I'm done!" Or maybe she has never spent the day sitting in a pediatric waiting room and feeling like a leper because she has to sit on the "sick kids" side. ("You would have to be an awfully impotent germ not to be able to make it fifteen feet across a room," I often grumble to myself on such occasions.) But I know she has. After all, she is a mother, isn't she? And yet, she is able to have fun with her children, freely, openly, totally.

Last winter this woman planted an indoor garden with her children, and spent hours playing with carrot tops and sweet potatoes. And she didn't even consider asking her doctor for a tranquilizer on the day when her five-year-old learned to use the telephone by calling a playground in Alaska. "Parenting is an occupation," she contends, "a total commitment, not just a sideline."

Many of us simply don't have this much time or patience to give to our children. But that doesn't mean we can't learn how to enjoy them more. It doesn't mean we can't learn how to add more quality to the time we do spend with them.

Quality Time: The Contemporary Panacea

The term *quality time* is really getting a workout in our modern-day world, although it is a term that just came into being about ten years ago when psychologists began using it to distinguish between giving real attention to a child and just sitting in the same room with him. Maybe we are fooling ourselves into believing that quality without quantity can be enough. Or maybe we will someday find out that it was enough after all. At any rate, for various reasons (some, but not all, of which are beyond our control), each parent has only a certain number of hours to spend with his family. It is the parent's job to make that precious time as special as possible.

Some research studies have revealed that mothers who stay home with their children only spend about one-half hour a day actually playing with those children. On the other hand, however, a mother who comes home from work exhausted every night doesn't have much quality left in her to give to anyone.

Most people believe that each individual has to find the balance between the intentional times planned into a schedule to be with one's children (I still remember where my parents sat at my third-grade school play, even though I can't remember whether I got the part of the elm tree or the holly bush) and the magic moments that just happen when parents and children simply "hang around" together ("Can I bring my book in here and sit and read with you?" Becky recently asked me, with as much excitement as if I had just offered her two expense-paid weeks in Disney World).

Spending quality time with one's children should involve spending the kind of time together that will be pleasant for both the parent and the child. But it doesn't always work out that way. I, for example, have spent quite a few nights in a sleeping bag, even though I know full well I could never look like I am enjoying myself sleeping in anything that even faintly resembles a tent. I once heard Joan Rivers say her idea of roughing it is when room service doesn't answer until the third ring. I couldn't agree more. Someday, I am going to get that point across to my daughter.

The parents who have had the most luck at planning build-your-own-adventure quality time with their children are the parents who have been open and honest about their own preferences. Some of them have told me that they have signed up for family gym programs at the Y, or gone on family hikes during which they have collected flowers and leaves for display, or built tree houses with their children, or helped those children plan backyard art shows or dramas. And they did it because they enjoy doing these things.

Other parents remember, with much fondness, the time when they played church with a sick child on Sunday morning or read a story backwards with their children or allowed a son or daughter to add up the grocery bill on a calculator during an afternoon at the supermarket.

All such parents work hard to stay attuned to the times when their children need them the most. I even read about one busy working mother who, having noticed that her child needed to spend some time with her, canceled all her appointments and sent a written excuse to the child's school explaining that the child would be spending the day playing with Mommy. Needless to say, this turned out to be a very special quality time.

"What are you saving your good china and towels for?" someone once asked me, and I suddenly realized I didn't have an
answer. A visit from a rich uncle I never knew I had? A dowry
for my daughter, perhaps? (No way. Especially after she asked
me last week if she could have my powder-blue sweater when I
get too old to wear it.) Although, I didn't have an answer for
my friend's question, it did cause me to ask myself another question: Why are you afraid to plunge yourself into life, to taste its
fullness, to live each day as a unique, never-to-be-reclaimed, God-
given opportunity for joy and growth?

As a result, I've really decided to relax and get more out of
life this year . . . to spend a few more hours dangling my feet
in the lake with my family . . . to stop letting little things annoy
me so much. In short, I've decided to improve the quality of
my life, and by doing that, I can't help but improve the quality
of time spent with my children.

Utilizing the Priceless Gift of Humor

"One day I woke up and realized I was the mother of four
kids, all under the age of five," sighed a friend. "That is when I
decided I had to start laughing or I wasn't going to survive."

I know exactly what she means. A good laugh has gotten me
through some of life's toughest moments. Just the other day, in
fact, when I read that I had already entered my mid-life crisis
and was fast approaching my sexual peak, I laughed to keep
from crying.

Laughter does have some therapeutic benefits. It reduces stress,
helps us communicate with each other, and causes us to look
at life in a more positive manner. Of course, this doesn't mean
that we can never be serious, or that we can laugh all our troubles
away. Neither does it mean that we should use our sense of
humor to put other people down, to hint that our children are
fat or dumb or cowardly—nor does it mean that everyone is
going to love a practical joker who sees great humor in hiding
his pet mouse in someone's best casserole dish. Instead, the truth
is found in the simple fact that a good sense of humor can make
life a lot more fun.

"Before you can use your sense of humor, you first have to
accept the fact that your kids are eventually going to find a totally

inappropriate time and place to tell everything they know," commented a mother who has been burned, "but the trouble is they often think they know things that they don't really know." This woman's young son had gone to school one day and informed his teacher that his daddy wasn't sleeping with his mommy anymore. All because the father had once come home from a business trip in the middle of the night and collapsed on the living room couch.

Young children also have the exasperating habit of never knowing when to speak and when to refrain from speaking. One of my friends found this out when she read the story of Bucky Beaver to her children (complete with an exaggerated impersonation of the buck-toothed little darling) and then took them out for an ice-cream soda. "While we were sitting in the soda shop that afternoon in walked the woman who was president of everything in town," my friend explained. Unfortunately, this influential woman also had a very pronounced overbite.

"What a happy little group," the woman smiled when she saw the children devouring their treats, and the children's mother was caught in the middle of one of those moments when you suddenly see a tractor trailer coming straight at you at top speed and know it's too late to do anything about it.

"Oh, Bucky!" one of the children cried with glee.

"Just like Bucky Beaver," the other joined in. "Can we take her home with us, Mommy?"

But Mommy didn't answer. It's hard to answer questions when you are lying under a soda shop table in a dead faint.

During times like these, you have little choice but to turn to your sense of humor, even though you know there are people involved who are not going to find the experience funny at all. Of course, it also helps to remind yourself that you can't expect adult behavior out of someone who doesn't even know how to tie his shoes yet. And it helps to tell yourself that things could be worse. After all, you could have been chosen chaperone for this month's Girl Scout hiking trip.

Using your sense of humor is one thing. Understanding your child's sense of humor is quite another. I'm not even sure it is possible to laugh with someone whose idea of humor is watching his brother fall down the stairs—or seeing his best friend throw up in gym class.

Children do love to feel included in family jokes, though, almost as much as they love to be tickled and wrestled to the floor. They like to feel as if they are part of the "group," and family jokes have a way of promoting this kind of feeling.

Many people cannot even remember how most of their family jokes got started. I know I can't. My father and I had a running joke going for years, the punch line of which was the question, "How?" And the answer was, "Fried." Eventually, I forgot the joke altogether. I think it had something to do with an Indian and an egg, but I'm not sure. Nevertheless, my father and I continued to try to catch each other off guard with the question, "How?" just to see if the other person would remember to answer, "Fried."

This running joke went on during my dad's entire life. Sometimes, I would get letters in the mail, even after I was married, entire sheets of stationery with nothing on them but the word, "How?" Other times, it would be a one-word long-distance phone call or a cassette tape. I told the non-joke to Becky one day, and she thinks it is hysterical. And so, the tradition goes on. But how many other people are going to find anything amusing in all this—or even be persuaded to believe that a normal, intelligent, college-educated bunch of people could sit around saying, "How?" to each other and then break into peals of laughter because of it?

Oh well, it's funnier than a lot of jokes Becky and her friends tell me. In fact, I've tried, over and over, to find humor in a seven-year-old's jokes, only to end up wondering how long you can laugh when your daughter tells you the kids at school voted her joke the best joke of the year, and then proceeds to tell it to you like this: "Question: What did one balloon say to the other balloon? Answer: Nothing. Balloons can't talk."

I may not find my child's jokes to be very funny, but I do find a lot of what she says to be absolutely hilarious, particularly when she doesn't mean for it to be. Like the time she pronounced her bride and groom paper dolls man and wife "with liberty and justice for all." Or the time she asked me why we sing "Hark! the Herald Angels Sing" at church when Harold was the bad guy who wanted to kill Jesus.

I've also found that I need to call upon my sense of humor when I am spending time with groups of children—teaching a Church School class, for instance. Sometimes though, I have to think of the children's best interests and hold my chuckles until I get home. Like I did the morning I checked my students' memory work. "And what is the ninth commandment, Mary?" I asked one of my best pupils.

"Thou shalt not lie down and bear false witness," she recited, in a confident voice. That was the same week I heard another kid singing "Joshua fit the battle of Geritol" during opening exercises.

Another time when a sense of humor comes in handy is when you are helping your child with his homework. For, it can be pretty embarrassing to discover you don't know the answers to three of the level-one questions. I figure your only hope is to try to laugh your way out of that sort of thing. Either that or put your spouse in charge of homework.

Life with Children, and Other Major Embarrassments

Young children have a knack of being able to turn just about anything into an embarrassing situation. And we never know when they are going to strike, so we always have to be prepared.

Judith Viorst once devoted her entire column in *Redbook* magazine to citing people's most embarrassing moments. Not surprisingly, many of these involved children—children who use the display toilets in department stores, for example, and children who ask, during a solemn Mass, why the priest is wearing a flea collar. One mother even told about someone asking her preschool daughter how she, the only girl in the family, happened to get three brothers. "Well, my mommy says that when Daddy goes to bed he leaves his motor running," the little girl replied. "And when daddies leave their motors running, that's what happens."[3]

I have a friend who remembers a moment with her children that was both embarrassing and near-disastrous. It happened the year her family spent Christmas at her brother-in-law's house. "It had taken them three years to furnish that new home," this woman explained, "and everything was so beautiful; but I should have been looking at my son, not at the house." Especially when her son opened his favorite Christmas gift—a tool kit.

The little boy had asked his older brother to read the tool kit directions to him, directions which merely said, "Carefully hold the handle of the saw, and saw back and forth." The boy's mother was lucky enough that day to walk into her brother-in-law's family room just in time to see her son's new saw coming down across an antique marble-top table.

I've had my embarrassing moments, too. The day I was giving a new church member a tour of our church day nursery, for example, just in time to hear one of the teachers saying to a child, "I know you made it, but you must not put your hands in the toilet." Or the time when I was entertaining some very sophisticated company and Becky suddenly discovered that one of the books she was reading made reference to a "poop deck."

Even life's embarrassing moments can be savored by someone with a good sense of humor. If they aren't too embarrassing, that is. . . . Is your child's humor too sarcastic? Maybe there is a truth in there somewhere that he is trying to reveal. Are his silly jokes played on other people too frequently? If so, then it could be a plea for more attention. The wise parent is also the perceptive parent.

It also helps to remember that even God, although He loves us totally, doesn't laugh at everything we do. But He always listens to us. He always stands ready to help us break through our facades. He is always prepared to teach us how to make our lives richer, fuller, more fun. And therein, once again, lies our perfect parental model.

Parting Tips

When you don't feel like laughing . . .

—If your child tells a joke that isn't funny at all, but doesn't have anything to do with personal injuries or bodily functions, laugh anyway. Loud.

—Try to pep up your life by catching a favorite old movie on TV—or by rearranging the furniture. A Charles Schulz cartoon puts it another way, "Decorate your home. It gives the illusion that your life is more interesting than it really is."

—Count your blessings. And tell yourself that the kids won't be bed-wetters forever.

—Ask yourself, often, if you are truly living every day of your life.

—Protect your sense of humor. Nurture it. Even when you don't feel like it. I have a hunch that we who are still parents of grade-school children are going to need our sense of humor a lot more later on.

10

How to Have the Kind of Home You Want

Joy in the Family Setting

"A dry crust eaten in peace is better than steak every day along with argument and strife."

— Proverbs 17:1, TLB

"The trouble with many of today's Christian homes is that a lot of people think of their children as a kind of necessary nuisance," a minister once told me. "It's a sort of 'you have to have kids whether you want to or not because God said you did' mentality."

Thus, we have the young, starry-eyed newlyweds who are sure they can live out their entire threescore and ten years together on little more than wedding cake and moonlight. Certainly they will live happily ever after. It is the way life is supposed to be for those who play the game right. People get married, love each other, give birth to children, and have a blast.

That is the fantasy world. What really happens is that you start out with two big people who get used to spending at least a couple of nights a week lying in front of a cozy fire and making love. Then, you add in two or three little people who live their lives for the sole purpose of finding ways to crawl between the two big people and throw a pair of wet socks into the fire. Now, you have two big people who must discover a way to deal with the fact that they are responsible for bringing into the world these little people who are, above all else, out to spoil their fun.

119

"It wasn't supposed to turn out this way," the couple cry out, but they never thought of asking anyone who really knew. Now they are no longer merely husband and wife; they are also father and mother. And their primary relationship is bound to begin suffering some neglect at this stage in their lives simply because of the amount of energy they are suddenly being forced to expend in the direction of their children. "The main reason parents of young children are not able to do everything right is that they are in a constant state of aggravation," one father told me.

That is the dark side. But you'll be glad to know that it isn't the only side. At least not for those parents who are willing to accept the fact that married life with children is going to be somewhat different than married life without them. Not necessarily worse. Just different. What that difference will entail is dependent, to a large extent, upon the parents themselves.

Fun in the Wading Pool

First, it is probably necessary for us to accept the fact, once and for all, that real families are not like "The Brady Bunch." Real families are a lot less sure of themselves—and they are a lot messier. "In order for something to become clean," insists one of Murphy's Laws, "something else must become dirty." Having children around the house makes you feel like you should have this law engraved on your doorpost.

I used to think I could pattern my home after the one on "The Brady Bunch." "After all," I reasoned, "Mrs. Brady has six children, and I only have one. It should be a snap." But I had forgotten that those people had to stay clean and beautiful and happy only as long as they were in front of a TV camera. They had a crew of designers and make-up artists and stage technicians to help them do it, too. And they even got weekends off. Besides, they were getting paid to keep their lives in order. I wasn't getting paid for anything.

Soon, I started to see more and more dissimilarities. My daughter began to openly declare her mother's stupidity, for example. "That's groceries," she would respond to all of my ideas. (The children at her school had gotten tired of the word *gross,* so they had begun substituting the word *groceries.*)

"Marsha Brady would never have said that," I would think to myself.

Then one day Becky was throwing a fit, yelling at her father, threatening never to speak to him again. "Let me have that in writing, and I'll leave you alone," I heard Revis yell back.

"Mr. Brady would never have said that," I thought to myself once again.

That is when I gave up hope—and I let things begin to deteriorate around me. "I think I'll go outside and chop down a dog house," Becky told me one day.

"That's nice, dear," I heard myself reply.

Luckily, she got involved in a neighborhood game of horseshoes instead, but I shouldn't have given up so easily. Not that I should have held onto my elusive dreams of mothering the world's first perfect family, but I should have searched deeper. I should have been able to see that it really is possible to have something that is very close to the kind of home you truly want to have. Now I know better. A little better, at least.

In Pursuit of the Happy Family

A few years ago, two professors at the University of Nebraska conducted a study of 350 families. According to their findings, happy families tend to exhibit several similar characteristics. They spend time together and communicate well; they appreciate each other and remain committed to each other, even to the extent of being able to find something positive to hang on to in the midst of crises. Most of the happy families surveyed were actively religious; many shared regular prayer and Bible reading experiences in their homes.[4]

I've always believed that family dinner table conversation can reveal a lot about a family's happiness, as families toss around their ideas and talk about their days. Of course, when the children are very young, there are bound to be times when such conversation reveals little more than the fact that the youngsters prefer Big Macs to Mom's beef stroganoff.

There will also be times when your dinner table conversation will convince you that the producers of green vegetables had better not depend on your family to keep their businesses afloat. ("I always told my kids, 'A teaspoonful of mud wouldn't kill you,' when I was trying to get them to eat their vegetables," one mother explained, "because I figured even Brussels sprouts wouldn't taste as bad as mud.")

Then there is the problem of sound effects at mealtime. You get a whole lot of that when there are young children at the table. Sometimes it's almost like being at a dinner theater—a dinner theater, that is, where the show that is playing is *The Three Stooges Talk Back to Their Food*. And yet, as long as you're prepared for all this, most parents insist, you won't feel impossibly frustrated.

Thus, doing everything possible to share the evening meal together as a family is usually worth the trouble in the long run. For the working mother, it might even be her only chance to learn what happened at school that day. And how could anyone make it through life without knowing that the star of last year's church Christmas pageant got sent to the principal's office because she brought an anatomically correct doll to school? Besides, dinner table conversation has long been accepted as one of the contributing factors involved in building healthy family relationships.

There are other factors, too. According to an article in *Parents* magazine, Dr. Robert Beavers, a professor at the University of Texas Health Center, believes that family negotiation may be the single most important one. The idea, then, is that, while both parents work together as a team, the entire family needs to learn how to compromise—that is, to settle differences by each side making concessions. It is not like the cartoon that pictures two little boys in a wagon with one saying to the other, "One of us would have a lot more fun if you would get out and push." It is more like taking turns pushing. Of course, it also makes sense to expect some conflict within a family situation.

When you become a parent, you are suddenly living with at least one small, but loud, person who spends almost as much time upside down as he does right side up (often in more ways than one). You may also be living in the kind of home where, as one mother put it, "There is a Muck Monster living under the rug in the basement laundry room, and he demands socks as tribute, but never two of the same pair." Living in the midst of such a world requires a lot of patience and understanding.

Letting the Good Words Roll

Happy families don't always agree on everything, but they do have constructive ways of handling their conflicts. They don't let the little irritations of life build up to explosive levels either, and they know how to display the age old virtues of courtesy and kindness.

"Ellen, would you please hand me that spoon?" Crash! "Oh, don't think a thing about it. That cream pitcher is so old I'm almost glad you broke it."

That is the way I would talk to one of my friends.

"Becky, get me that spoon. Hurry up. You'd think I never taught you how to walk." Crash! "Ahhhhggg, not the cream pitcher. Get out of here. Now! And don't expect me to pay to get your ears pierced. You've already got more than enough holes in your head."

That is the way I would talk to my daughter, at least on those days when I am in my true motherhood form.

Recently, I read about an exercise often used in parenting workshops. Families are asked to list phrases they most and least like to hear. In a study of seventy-five fourth and fifth graders, the phrases these children said they most like to hear from their mothers are "I love you," "time to eat," and "you can go." One parent could hardly believe it when his children listed the phrases they most commonly hear at home and included statements like, "What's on?" and, "Move."[5]

There are times when I feel that the phrase I am hearing most often in my own house is "I can take care of myself." And, I feel that, no matter what I do, I am going to keep on hearing it—at least until Becky grows up and starts looking for somewhere to send her own kids for school vacations. But then I could be wrong. Because I also think my husband should know when I need my back rubbed without my having to tell him.

Family members need to talk to each other and tell each other how they feel and what they want. They need to balance their needs for separation and togetherness, and they need to receive verbal affirmation from each other—words of support and encouragement. This is not news, and few people have any trouble agreeing with it. The trouble comes when we try to put it into practice.

Members of a family have to know each other before they can genuinely affirm each other. They have to spend a lot of time building relationships with each other before they can be there for each other when one of them is in need.

"I spent hours punishing Michael before I truly got to know him," one parent told me, "but eventually I came to see that my other two kids are the type who could spend the day passing notes back and forth in class, while Michael is the type who could pass only one note in his entire life; and he would get caught." There are kids like that. They watch the other kids sneak into the new camp counselor's cabin and initiate his belongings with a can of shaving cream—and then they end up in the camp infirmary awaiting sentence while being treated for an allergy to an ingredient in the cream. In order to have the kind of homes we want, we have to understand our children.

Many people contend that family members could get to know each other much better if they limited their TV viewing. I think they are probably right. I'll never forget the night the TV set broke at our house. Becky was about three at the time, and she spent the evening saying, "What was that? Did you hear that?" It was an astonishing night of discovery for her because she had never before known that a heat pump cuts on and off or a refrigerator crackles or a house settles. Now these may not seem like monumental discoveries to you and me. Certainly nothing that would win anyone a Nobel Prize—or even be worth a guest spot on "20/20." But a three-year-old needs to know the world is something more than what she sees on TV.

Children need to feel secure within their families. It often helps them to know that they have extended families, too. Unfortunately though, the life of mobility that most of us now lead can easily rob our children of the benefits of spending time with their grandparents.

"Do you know that Grandma still has that dumb old picture of Donald Duck that I drew when I was four?" Becky asked me during one of our visits to Grandma's house in Illinois.

"I'm not surprised," I smiled. "She still has all of my first grade papers."

"Really?" my daughter exclaimed. "Grandma must really love us."

And that's just about it. Grandma really does love us—and Grandmas generally know how to love very well. On an episode of the TV show "Highway to Heaven," one of the characters was talking about our grandparents being like magic books that are filled with stories of who we are. The character went on to explain that, when those grandparents die, such stories are gone forever. We have to try, to the best of our abilities, not to deny our children their heritage. For, when we give our children the gift of heritage, we are giving them the opportunity to better understand themselves.

In Tune with the Children

Many parents have warned me not to expect too much out of a child too soon. For, while it is true that love and peace and harmony are contagious in a happy home, the incubation period may be longer for some children than for others. This is also true of passing along good habits.

One parent told me that she recently walked into her family room and noticed her child was watching something like *Godzilla Meets the Man in the Rubber Suit* on TV. He tried to convince her it was on an educational channel and that was the only reason he was watching it. Most parents have similar examples to share.

I spent one evening with a family who had decided to let their seven-year-old boy serve the cookies to their guests. The child seemed to be doing exceptionally well carrying the platter around, so much better than the night when he had poured a glass of Pepsi down a company president's Aigner tie. So no one even realized, for quite a while, that the boy was taking the cookies off the platter with his fingers and placing them on each person's plate.

It reminded me of the night I caught Becky licking all the cookies at the church social so that she could be sure to select the best tasting ones . . . or the day I spent so many hours teaching my child how to act as a guide for guests at our open house and then heard her leading people from room to room and pointing out all of our wastebaskets to them. ("And this is my mom and dad's trash can.")

And yet, we must never despair. For, we can be assured that our children finally will grow up and learn how to behave with at least enough of a touch of etiquette to earn them the right to go wherever they really want to go. They will someday develop a true sense of family, too, if we take the time to show them that family is a high priority in our own lives.

I have no doubt that my best memories, the times I am going to be able to close my eyes and see forty years from now, will be those that involve my family having fun together. I know several families who go bike riding together regularly and others who make children's sports events family affairs, with Dad as coach and Mom as head cheerleader (or vice versa). "No one takes home movies of the family doing dishes or making beds," one of these family members emphasized, "but it is true that you may have to buy your fun at the expense of reducing your expectations about housework and other time-consuming activities."

Our culture is a time-oriented culture. Much of the life within it is structured around duty and schedule. "The thing that used to hurt me the most when my kids were growing up," admitted one father, "were the nights when I would come home from work late and see my son sitting on the front porch holding his baseball glove and my baseball glove—and there would be only thirty minutes left until dark." Often, there has to be something almost sacrificial involved in giving one's children a sense of family.

At the same time, however, there are many parents among us who try too hard. Joseph Procaccini, an authority on family relationships at Loyola College, insists that as many as 50 percent of today's parents are experiencing, at least to some extent, what he refers to as "parent burnout." Such parents are trying too hard to be perfect, asking themselves too often, "What did I do wrong?" These individuals are generally well educated, highly motivated, middle class people who are either past or future oriented and who try to "control" their children, but who eventually feel smothered by their parental responsibilities. Professor Procaccini advises parents who are feeling the squeeze to remember that, much of the time, "raising a family is like trying to hit a moving target."[6] How true that is.

"Just when I thought I had figured out how to have a peaceful, harmonious Christian home," one mother sighed, "my youngest son decided he wanted to learn how to play the trumpet." Life is like that, in many different ways; and the parent who learns to roll with the punches and keep plugging away in spite of those punches is the parent who has a real chance of coming out ahead in the end.

A House Not Divided

In Matthew 12:25, we are told that a house divided cannot stand. But how can we keep our houses from getting divided? What chance do we have in this world in which we live, a world where everything seems to be working against us?

"I've learned not to be too surprised when people get divorced," a friend recently told me, "but when a member of my mother's senior citizens' craft group divorced her husband after fifty-two years of marriage . . . well, I still haven't recovered from that one."

Healthy spouses complement each other, according to Dr. Jerry J. Lewis, who wrote a book on families entitled *No Single Thread;* and children in healthy families have no question about which parent is boss because they know that both parents are. I think we can take that idea even one step further and say that, in a Christian home, the family members know that neither the husband nor the wife is the head of the house because God is.

We are told, in Psalm 127, "Unless the Lord builds the house, its builders will have toiled in vain" (NEB). And where God is, there also is love. But we still have to find ways to show that love to each other. "How I yearned for love to be demonstrated in the home where I grew up," one woman told me, "but I was never sure I was loved because no one ever kissed me or told me so." The year before her mother died, this woman finally got up the courage to tell her mother how she felt; and, during their last year together, mother and daughter shared a relationship that was more beautiful than either of them had ever dreamed it could be.

Ministers throughout the country advise their congregations, week after week, to allow God to show them how to demonstrate love to the members of their families—by working at it and by experiencing God's own unconditional acceptance of His children. "We are constantly trying to make each other into what we imagine the other person to be," one parent told me. "We do this with our children, and we do it with our spouses, certain that we can find a way to mold each person into a different image instead of accepting the God-given image that each already projects and doing our best with whatever that might be."

Our families are important—critically important, not only to us, but also to the other families around us. Over and over again, people tell me that they truly believe this. They believe we can have the kinds of homes we want. They believe in the future of America's Christian families—as we love and grow together and, thus, build the kind of world we have always hoped to pass on to the generations of families to come after us.

Parting Tips

When you are trying to build the kind of home you want . . .

—Take off the masks. You can't fool someone who lives with you, even if she is only six years old. Maybe especially if she is only six years old.

—Tune up your parenting skills. Read books. Take courses if necessary. Parenting is the hardest job in the world, and the best preparation most of us ever get for it is on-the-job self-training.

—Involve your children in the family's decision-making process. This helps prevent the playing off of one parent against another, particularly since all parents like to create the illusion that they are smarter than their children, at least until the children make it through grade school.

—Share your feelings—and your physical affection—with other members of your family. "I'm lonely. Can I snuggle with you for a while?" one mother asked her five-year-old. The child was amazed that a mommy could feel lonely. He had always thought mothers were capable of displaying only three feelings—too busy, too tired, and too fat.

—Support church programs that strengthen family life. Christian families can be support groups for each other. And it never hurts to find out that you are not the only one ever to have a five-year-old who called the fire station and reported a fire at her house because her best friend got so much attention at school the week her house was robbed.

11

To Juggle or Not to Juggle

Family Life in Today's World

"You might as well curse your friend as wake him up early in the morning with a loud greeting."
—Proverbs 27:14, (TEV)

When my dad was a little boy, his mother used to take him and his nine brothers and sisters out to the back porch every Saturday night to give them baths. They were bathed in order of age from youngest to oldest. So, after the first two or three children, everyone else got mud baths. Only the baby got clean water. Well, sort of clean. Grandmother had already washed the clothes in the "bathtub" before she even got around to washing the children. ("Thank goodness we didn't use bleach in those days," one of my father's sisters recently told me.)

In today's world, it would be hard to imagine a typical American mother bathing ten children every Saturday night—and doing all the other weekday chores that such a family would demand. Of course, the ideal family size, even in 1945, still included at least four children. By 1980, that number was down to two.

Gone are the "good old days" when life revolved around family wiener roasts and hayrides and church meetings. "We used to have so much fun at our big family dinners," one grandmother told me, "but now when the kids and grandkids get together, we all go out to a restaurant because no one likes to cook anymore."

There is no longer a "typical American family" like there was in the 1950s. Back then, it consisted of a working father, a mother who stayed home, and one or more children, a seemingly workable mix which made up 70 percent of all American families. Less than 10 percent of today's families fit into that mold, mainly because of the drastic increase in single parent homes and working mothers.

According to Census Bureau projections, there will be 10.5 million working mothers of children under age six by 1990. And, if you want my already well-experienced opinion on this subject, not one of those mothers will be able to find a parking place . . . which brings me to the most significant question yet to be flung toward the twenty-first century: How in the world do today's Christian parents successfully juggle two careers, a busy church and community schedule, and the all-encompassing demands of a couple of squalling little munchkins without ever resorting to signing a check with a crayon? Or, do they?

Grand Central Station Was Never This Busy

It was almost 3:00 in the afternoon on an icy winter day, and my friend Jan was frantically working on an overdue order of craft items she supplies to a local boutique. She was behind because bad weather had intervened, and she had been called upon to drive her mother to a doctor's appointment that morning. Her spirits began to droop considerably when she looked at the clock and saw that it was almost time for her two youngest children to come home from school.

"Mom," her little girl screeched, as the back door slammed and the wet boots sloshed, "Mark hit Mr. Martin's window with a snowball."

"Slimy, little baby tattletale," growled Mark, as the next set of boots hit the linoleum. "Besides, it's just a little hole."

Mark was sent to his room to await the much overrated arrival of his father, and he didn't utter a single protest. "Why should he?" his mother thought to herself. "He could start his own Radio Shack franchise with the stuff he has accumulated in that room of his."

After that, things began to calm down a bit. Jan fixed her little girl an afternoon snack. ("No mushrooms in my hot chocolate today," requested the child, who had yet to learn the difference between the word *mushroom* and the word *marshmallow*.) Then, Jan continued working on her crafts. A few minutes later, however, her daughter inquired, as casually as any five-year-old would who barely has to lift a finger to do anything beyond finding the right TV channel for afternoon cartoons, "Mommy, what kind of cookies did you make for the PTO program tonight?"

"Cookies!" the mother exclaimed, with a depth of agony that would have been obvious to anyone who wasn't still five years old. "You didn't tell me anything about cookies!"

"Oh, didn't I give you that note? Oh, here it is. It must have gotten stuck on this sticky package of Twinkies in my school bag."

It was one of those not-so-rare moments when Mother was sure she would have thrown in the towel if she could have found a clean one. The charred remains of a pot of chili, which was supposed to have been dinner, sat on the stove threatening to set off the hallway smoke alarm. The dust on the refrigerator top was finally beginning to spill over onto the kitchen cabinets. And, poor Jan's teen-age daughter had chosen that very moment to glide into the house and announce, in what would pass for a sultry, R-rated whisper only to a seventeen-year-old, "Mother, Steve and I are thinking about getting engaged this Christmas."

The sad thing about all of this is that it was not such an unusual day in the life of my friend Jan. It might have been a little more extreme than her ordinary. But not much more. And Jan doesn't even have a full-time job.

According to data compiled from sources which include the Census Bureau, 78 percent of today's American women say their greatest problem in life is not having enough time. Clearly, one reason for this can be found in the fact that a full-time homemaker spends five to ten hours a day on housework, while a working wife still puts in four to eight hours a day keeping home and hearth in order. Liberated males, where are you when we really need you?

The Way It Is

Last month our church hosted an "old-fashioned box-lunch social." Everyone who planned to attend probably had visions of gingham tablecloths and oversized picnic baskets and home-baked brownies. But those visions were buried pretty deep in our subconscious minds, I guess. For, when the congregation of families was assembled that night, the big tables in the church foyer held at least two hundred boxes of *Kentucky Fried Chicken.*

Life is like that these days, even in the church, which is usually the last of the institutions to bend to the trappings of changing times. True, most of us have managed to achieve pretty good standards of living in today's world. (Ask us any time other than April 15, and we might even admit it.) And yet, it generally takes two good incomes to maintain such a standard of living. Thus, many young couples are now postponing parenthood, having fewer babies, and seldom letting their children become the central focus of their worlds.

One of the complexities arising out of all this is the fact that time pressure, emotional strain, and a sizable burden of guilt have already become gut-wrenching realities in the lives of most of today's mothers. Take my friend Pat, for example, who has her favorite Murphy's Law taped on her refrigerator door: "Whatever you want to do, you have to do something else first."

On the one hand, we have mothers insisting that they are great mothers only because they work, and that they would probably end up beating their kids if they didn't. (These mothers are generally biting their fingernails off even as they speak to you.) On the other hand, we have mothers assuring us that their children would grow up to be hardened criminals if they didn't stay home with the little darlings. (These mothers also tell you, with their eyes, that they will have *you* for dinner if you don't believe them.) Both kinds of mothers can find statistics to back up their individual stances in life. As usual, there has to be something between these two extremes.

I am acquainted with a fairly large number of latchkey children. Some of them seem to be doing very well. Others are so lonely that they flag down the ice cream truck even when they don't have any money just to have someone to listen to their jokes. Most of the time, I have no great desire to voice my opinions concerning the choices any of those children's parents have made (except maybe on those days when all the kids end up at my house with pets who couldn't be left home alone because they are being treated for some obscure flea disease—and with little

mouths that silently beg to be given just a little taste of the chocolate cake I made for that night's dinner). And yet . . .

"There are no set mealtimes at our home anymore," one extra
busy mother told me, "and everyone has been going in so many
different directions for so long now that I think I've already moved
beyond 'burnout' and made a premature arrival in 'rustout.'"

This is a common cry of anguish. Today's family doesn't know
what percentage of time to give anything anymore. Family members are involved in knothole games and ballet and Cub Scouts
and deacons' board and Rotary and countless other worthwhile
activities. But the problem is that too many worthwhile activities
can become too much for any one family to handle.

Recent studies completed by the National Institute of Education
and the Home and School Institute reveal that children of working
mothers do as well in school as children of nonworking mothers.
The study also points to the fact that the working mother spends
almost as much time caring for children as the at-home mother
does. (And then she undoubtedly collapses into a chair at the
end of each day and mumbles herself to sleep with the question,
"This is having it all? This is having it all?")

Maybe in all of this, there is a hint regarding the real trouble
we are seeing in many of today's families. Maybe we need to
find out where all of this child-care time is coming from. For,
it's not easy to be a parent, whether you work outside the home
or not; and it takes an enormous amount of time and energy
to come anywhere close to doing it right.

A short time ago, I walked into the supermarket just in time
to hear the clerks moaning and groaning. "What's wrong?" I
asked one of them.

"They're here again," she sighed, pointing in the direction of
a bunch of giggly teen-agers who had been sent out on a class
assignment from the local high school. They were supposed to
learn how to shop in a supermarket. "They even have a computer
back in the classroom that tells them how good they are going
to be at preparing a budget meal for a family of four," the clerk
whispered, "but I'll bet they don't have a computer that tells
them how to keep from looking like bag ladies while they're
cooking it."

"If they honestly want this to be realistic," I whispered back,
"they should put a couple of kids throwing temper tantrums into

each cart and then tell them they have to get to a committee meeting in ten minutes." But no one wants to be that realistic, I guess. Not even me.

How to Make It through the Morning in a Dual-Career Home

Each parent has his own personal tips about how to juggle various demands. Most of those tips, however, can be summed up in one word. That word is *compromise*—family compromise among couples, among parents and their children, among family members and people outside the home. Here are a few of the ways the parents I know have worked out their compromises.

Divisions of labor. Most of today's busiest families split the household chores among their members, at least to some extent. The wisest of these families try to match each specific chore to the person who does it best and likes it most. Of course, you are not going to find very many people who get too excited at the prospect of making a choice between taking out the garbage and cleaning the bathroom. In fact, you are probably better off if you don't have anyone that strange in your family.

One of my friend's kids recently asked to be paid for a newly selected chore—washing dishes. "I never got paid for washing dishes," my friend reminded her son, with an "I've got you this time" gleam in her eye.

"I know, Mom," the son replied, "but moms like doing dishes."

Anything you can do to streamline the housework will be greatly appreciated by the other members of your family. Maybe even appreciated enough so that your kids will get you something that doesn't glow in the dark for Christmas next year. Try an occasional picnic dinner with paper plates, for instance; and pur-. chase only easy-care clothing and household items—and, whatever you do, don't add any more dust-catching knickknacks to the family collection until you are less than three months away from cashing in your IRA.

Organizational tactics. Maybe you are not the kind of person who checks off daily chores in a spiral bound notebook, and files Campbell's Soup labels in an accordion file. Most of us aren't. I myself am much closer to the I'll-bet-that-floor-hasn't-been-scrubbed-in-two-months style. And yet, most of the parents who seem to be holding onto a measure of sanity will tell us they believe in being somewhat organized.

Some of them have put timers on their coffeepots and covered their doors with checklists for their children (Have you forgotten schoolbooks, mittens, your brains?). One mother borrowed a tip from a time management article and began using magnets to attach personalized envelopes containing lunch money, notes to the teacher, etc. to her refrigerator.

At the very least, most busy parents have learned to cook in quantity and freeze—everything from school lunches to today's equivalent of a company gourmet dinner. ("How about bringing the family over tonight and helping us find that Ziploc bag full of spaghetti I stored in the freezer?") A lot of these parents have also learned to use their time wisely in other areas of life by planning the day's activities around the times when they are most alert and energetic, for instance, or by using their commuting time to listen to tapes in the car.

All of us have the same number of hours to get everything done. Twenty-four each day, 168 each week, 8,736 each year. If we are able to use our organizational skills to save even fifteen minutes of that time each day, this amounts to an extra sixty hours a year to do what we want to do. Whatever we want to do . . . what a thought!

True, I would probably end up spending my extra time reading *The Little Engine That Could* to a kid who has already got it memorized—and getting so tired of the story that I would become tempted to read the last page wrong and tell my child that the little engine didn't make it after all because Amtrak went out of business and left the poor thing sitting on the railroad track in the snow starving to death. But maybe not. I might even get to use some of that time to lie on the patio and take that nap I've been promising myself ever since my oldest kid learned to feed herself.

The priorities that matter. "I love my career more than I could ever have imagined I would," a busy professional woman once told me, "but I never let myself forget, not even for a minute, that my greatest joy in life comes from relationships." This woman went on to say that she feels a great burden of sadness for the lack of relationship building in our society.

Parents need to spend time with their families. Even if it means compromising a few career options, even if it means letting the vacuuming go for another week. (One mother keeps her vacuum cleaner in the middle of the living room floor all the time so that anyone who drops by will think she was just getting ready to do the floors.) We need to be there often enough to savor the wonder of our children's growing-up years, to listen to their stories about the weird things other kids bring to school in their lunch boxes, even to make time to join them for lunch during their school's parent visitation week. (After all, how many other chances a year do you get to sit in a chair that barely holds a seven-year-old's bottom, eat mixed vegetables with a spoon, and listen to table conversation that revolves around hunting down dead mice?)

"Twenty years from now, you won't remember whether or not I ironed that shirt," my friend's mother once said to her, "but you just might remember that we went to the zoo today, and I don't ever want to feel like I let a date with a can of spray starch keep me from making you a memory."

Many Christian parents have told me that the successful balance of their days has a direct correlation to their relationships with God. If they don't make time for their devotional lives, they find that they soon have little energy for anything else. If they start confusing the busy-work of church activities with the call from God to build a family, they quickly find themselves unable to be of real service to anyone. The true success, they insist, comes as a result of putting first things first.

It isn't always easy to put first things first. Just as it isn't always easy to wake up and face a new day of juggling. Sometimes we even have lapses, and we go overboard. Like the mother who once became so obsessed with having a perfectly organized, spotless home that she began handing toys out the window to her children to keep the floors clean. The day she caught herself thinking about ridding her house of dirt by removing all the flowerpots she snapped out of it and began her trek back toward real life.

Real life—where little children create elaborate, dripping mud pies and carry them across the carpet to present them to their parents, fully expecting nothing short of a blue ribbon in return. Real life—where a mother hears her child, on his way in from art class, being told by his father, "Be careful now until you get into the house. I don't want you to spill all that in my garage."

My friend Mimi once took the whole organization thing to extremes. She did this, she told me, because for the past twenty years, Christmas had come too fast for her. Every year she would find herself rushing out of the house clutching forgotten lists, hoping against hope that the drugstore would still be open at 6:00 P.M. on Christmas Eve. And so, she decided, finally, that she would organize her Christmas holiday.

I'll never forget how proudly Mimi told me about all of her gifts being neatly wrapped and ready to go—so early. Too early, as it turned out. For, when Mimi carried her carefully prepared treasures down the stairs on Christmas Eve night, the tape on every package broke.

Yes, no matter how well we plan and organize our days, life has a way of throwing us an occasional curve ball, at least in part, simply because we are parents. Just think, for example, of the fact that the average child under age seven gets two to seven colds or flu viruses each winter. (Any child on the low end of that spectrum is probably a candidate for *Ripley's Believe It or Not.*) It doesn't take much more than a little fact like that to put a pretty big dent into a perfectly planned day.

Thus, the best advice I ever got from anyone on the subject of juggling activities and time was the suggestion to plan my time wisely, but keep my plans flexible. When I became a mother, I learned that I must not take my well-planned life too seriously either. I found that one out the day Becky's elementary school class was studying their parents' careers.

I fully expected my child to come home that day with flowery tales about her father's earthshaking sermons and important work for our state denominational headquarters—and about her mother's fascinating travels as a department store buyer which one day gave way to a budding career built around writing books that are surely bound for the best-seller list.

"What did you tell the people at school about your mom and dad's occupations?" I asked my child, my heart almost pounding.

"Oh, I just told them my mom used to sell stuff in a store, but now she just sits around the house and writes in her diary a lot. Then, I told them my dad cleans up around a church."

And the juggling goes on.

Parting Tips

When you are juggling too many things . . .

—Brush up on your organizational skills, and force yourself to say no when you feel that you should. Make checklists, but don't expect to get everything done. Any kid worth the label has a sixth sense for knowing the worst possible time to bring home three hungry friends.

—Know your options when it comes to child care. Job sharing and flex-time are becoming more popular in some fields; and, even those couples who work full time outside the home don't have to select the first day-care alternative that arises. Talk to friends. Shop around. Learn how to spot red flags. Avoid seriously considering a day-care center if, when you visit it and ask to see the children, no one can find them.

—Take your child along to visit your place of employment. Preferably on a day when his nose isn't running enough to make him look contagious.

—If you decide to start collecting anything during these years, try quick-cook menus—and hints on how to keep your child from hacking away at your good name in the community while you are at work.

—Analyze your activities. Even if you are not involved in a career, you are probably an extremely busy person. Make sure your activities fit in with your priorities, your goals, and your time schedule. Don't sign up for a class in bread baking if you can't even find the time to get to the store to buy a loaf—and don't do anything that will keep you from sharing a quiet time each day with God.

12

Of Personal Growth among Parents . . . and Other Impossible Dreams

Societal Roles and Today's Parents

"It is better—much better—to have wisdom and knowledge than gold and silver."

—Proverbs 16:16, TEV

This morning Becky strutted off to school wearing her favorite message T-shirt. "Let's face it," the message reads, "girls are smarter." I must admit that I sent her off with more than one second thought, wondering if she would come home with her first black eye, or, even worse, with a note reprimanding her mother—and asking me to staff the sponge-throw booth at next week's school Fun Day.

For a moment, I guess I had forgotten that this is the same child who has waked up every morning during her entire eight years of life and focused her eyes on a plaque that hangs on the wall in front of her bed. Its message? "Girls can do anything." My daughter is a child who can take care of herself. I shouldn't have worried.

When Becky came home from school this afternoon, she told me that most of the boys didn't pay much attention to her message because "they are used to stuff like that." One boy (whose father is a truck driver) did challenge her to a math contest; but she won, so he didn't say anything more. Her favorite boyfriend in class had even complimented her on the shirt. (Too much in love and still too far removed from the altar to care about its implications, no doubt.)

Why was I surprised? Today's attitudes toward male and female roles in society are vastly different from the ones that existed even during my generation's growing-up years. "Can you believe my high school offered driver's education only to boys?" one of my friends asked me. And, in a recent magazine article, I read about a woman physician asking her little boy if he would someday like to be a doctor only to be informed that he didn't think he could because he was a boy. Even I, though I was always sure I knew how to use all the right terms, have been taken to task in regard to today's new vocabulary.

"Let's go outside and build a snowman," I suggested to Becky last week.

"Mom," she chastised, "it's snowperson."

And I certainly never thought a thing about singing "Peace on earth, good will to men" at Christmas time until my daughter began chanting, "Peace on earth good will to girls."

Man, Woman, Equality, and Whatever Happens Next

Introducing today's father—a man who will not only sit through a kindergarten parent-teacher conference, but will also tell the guys at work about it . . . and today's mother—a woman who insists that a real mom doesn't need to spend her afternoons sitting home indexing her collection of recycled aluminum foil and used grocery bags. About the only thing you can say to describe these individuals is they don't fit well into molds anymore. Let's take a look at each of them individually.

Gentlemen first. Many people believe that today's lifestyle is hard on men. Certainly, there are no longer any clear stereotypes for them to fall back on, no easy rules, cast in concrete. (They aren't even the only ones mixing the concrete anymore.) And yet, just because something is more difficult doesn't necessarily make it worse. Most often, in fact, our struggles in life are what cause us to grow into better people.

Large numbers of today's males are not at all dissatisfied with their expanded roles at home. And research from the United States government and other agencies reveals that men are not totally shirking their responsibilities when it comes to the dreaded household chores either. For, at least occasionally, 56 percent of the males recently surveyed do the major grocery shopping, 47 percent vacuum, 44 percent cook complete meals, and 41 percent wash dishes.

"Occasionally" may not sound good enough to some of the women who would rather have two extra Pap smears a year than spend another evening with a scouring pad, but it's certainly a step beyond the old days of slippers and pipes and "Yes dear, you really did beat me at tennis fair and square."

When it comes to the subject of child care, today's men seem to be even more enthusiastic. U.S. government research reveals that 75 percent of them say they would make at least one career sacrifice in order to have and raise children. And an extensive research study tosses in the information that eight out of ten men agree that, when both parents work, each should play an equal role in child care.

Such has not always been the case. I remember my own father standing incognito in the lobby at one of my dance recitals. He spent the night slouching around the walls like a bum looking for somewhere to get rolled, with his hat pulled down so far he could have made it into the Charlie Daniels Band.

And then there was my girl friend's dad, who was convinced that he would catch some terrible disease that would stop hair from growing on his face and raise his voice two octaves if he ever tried feeding or diapering his new baby daughter. "When that baby is tall enough to see over my shoulder, I'll start talking to her," he always chuckled, obviously forgetting that children don't talk at that age, but, rather, merely mumble an infrequent, incomprehensible word about needing money for gas.

Even my own husband was something of a question mark in my mind before Becky was born. After all, he had been raised on a farm, proud that he could plow a field at age nine and fit in with the tobacco-spitting locals at the R & R Cafe at age thirteen. Clearly not the type a woman would be anxious to show off at the state ERA meeting. Maybe that is why the letter that Revis wrote to Becky the night before we brought her home from the hospital still qualifies as one of the greatest personal revelations of my life.

"I see not the fulfilling of my dreams in giving you life," he wrote, "but the beginning of those dreams. For, you are my daughter, and I am your father. I don't know you yet, but somehow I've known you all along. We will learn of each other, how to care and live and love. I think you already know how to love as you lie curled up in my arms. Teach me to love you."

According to a survey released a short time ago by the American College of Obstetricians and Gynecologists, four out of five fathers are now present at the delivery of their children. Today's men attend childbirth classes with their wives and go to prenatal appointments at the doctors' offices. Nearly 100 percent of them help with the baby at home. Three-fourths change diapers, two-thirds help with the feedings, and more than 40 percent bathe their babies.

We've come a long way from the day of my birth, the day when my mother spoke those fateful words that linked her so tightly with the women of her generation. "Just put me out, doctor," she said. "I don't want to know what's happening, and I don't want to see my husband again for at least six years."

But what about those men who are still having trouble defining their roles in the home? Men who tell me they know they are missing the boat with their children, but don't know what to do about it. Men who can't help feeling that there is something almost poetic in the idea that *Real Men Don't Eat Quiche,* and in the book of that same title which speaks of the "real man" in this way: ". . . he realizes that while birds, flowers, poetry, and small children do not add to the quality of life in quite the same manner as a Super Bowl, . . . he's learned to appreciate them anyway."[7]

Such men probably grew up among role models who held to the old-fashioned notion that a woman's place is in the house (certainly not, as today's popular saying goes, "and in the senate"). Most women who have husbands like this tell me they have had to take the lead when it comes to encouraging these men to become equal partners in the home.

"For years, I guarded my husband's free time from work and sheltered him from family turmoil," one woman explained, "and then, when the kids became teen-agers, he had to knock himself out to try to get to know them well enough to help them through their crises." This woman insists that her methods were off target.

"But I had been raised to believe that the house and children were exclusively my responsibility," she said. "I even thought it was all my fault each time I got pregnant."

"You can keep a husband from becoming a true helpmate in the home in all sorts of ways," another wife and mother remarked. Then she went on to talk about the night her husband decided to wash the dishes, and she walked into the kitchen just in time to inform him that his style of dish drying was all wrong. "He didn't say a word to me in response," she said. "He simply walked out the back door and broke every dish he had dried." It was a costly lesson, but one that any woman would find hard to forget.

In the book *What Is a Husband?*, one wife answered the question by explaining that a husband is a man who "stands by you through all the troubles you wouldn't have had if you had stayed single!" She is right, of course. But the statement is also true in reverse: A wife is a woman who "stands by you through all the troubles you wouldn't have had if you had stayed single!" If my husband had remained single, he would never have had to warm a bottle or spend the night in a rocking chair. But he didn't remain single. And I, for one, am glad about that. He has discovered the importance of being a real father, too, and I have a feeling he is one among many on that score.

"I see an old man in my mind very often," a minister once told his congregation. "He is bent with the weight of many years. His head is crowned with a mantle of grey. He sits in a chair all the day long. Waiting out the twilight, reflecting, remembering, reliving his days. I want to be kind to that old man. I don't want to hurt him, or cause him to be filled with regret. For you see, that old man is me, forty, fifty, sixty years from now. He will be what I make him. He will have to live with what I do."[8]

Today's breed of father knows the value of active fathering. He knows he must fully assume his parental responsibilities if he is ever going to feel truly good about himself. He knows his involvement in the parenting process can bring joy and happiness to his whole family. But he also knows something else. He knows that, when he is with his children, he is where he honestly wants to be. There are even indications from some research studies that nurturing fathers help increase their children's scores on educational tests, and that many of today's successful women had strong, supportive dads.

A number of employers are still not making it easy for men to be involved in active parenting; but concerned fathers are managing, somehow, to be there anyway . . . in the pediatric waiting rooms, at the Girl Scout awards ceremonies, at the school pageants. For, these men believe, with a strength of character and a bravery of spirit that past generations might not have even labeled masculine, that this is where they truly belong.

Ladies' choice. Women talk a lot about personal fulfillment these days—and most of them find nothing particularly fulfilling about sitting around teaching their children how to make beautiful flower arrangements out of old Windex caps. I know how they feel. Before Becky was born, I even spent a lot of time worrying about what the label "mother" was going to do to my life. I knew I could never be Suzy Homemaker. That was for sure.

What I hadn't counted on was having a child who didn't care whether or not she had Suzy Homemaker for a mother. Thus, as I learned to plan the games for school parties and bake sheet cakes for church children's programs, I found my daughter to be a very undemanding accomplice.

I'll never forget the cupcakes I made for Becky's kindergarten party. She had requested them specifically—and Tootsie Roll Pops, too. The fact that I didn't own a muffin tin at the time meant little to me. I simply went out and bought some of those paper muffin cups and plopped them onto a cookie sheet. Somewhere along the way, I must have missed the Supermom 101 course where they teach you that cake dough expands when placed in an oven with nothing but a thin sheet of paper to stem the tide.

When it was all over, I pretended that the cupcakes looked just like I had intended them to look. After all, how many people get to eat something that looks like the aftermath of Hurricane Camille and call it a cupcake? Nothing like that for sheer excitement. Never mind that I had made matters worse by expecting a Tootsie Roll Pop to sit straight up, unassisted, in the middle of each cupcake.

"Maybe the children will think the suckers are the newest fad in creative eating utensils," I told myself. (Heaven knows, you would need some kind of utensil to eat such a soggy mess.) At any rate, Becky seemed to be genuinely impressed with my efforts.

In fact, it wasn't until almost a year later that I found out the truth.

It was trick-or-treat night, and I was taking my daughter around to friends' houses to collect her goodies. At one of the houses, I paused for a moment of conversation. "Becky wanted pumpkin cookies to take to school this year," I told my friend, "and I read the recipe wrong the first time around and had to make a whole new batch."

"Oh that's nothing," Becky interrupted. "You should have seen the cupcakes Mommy made for our kindergarten party last year. They were the most terrible looking things you have ever seen, but they tasted so good that the kids even asked for seconds."

Maybe getting it right as a mother doesn't have anything to do with getting it perfect after all. At least that's what I'm counting on. For, I truly believe you can take this perfect wife and mother thing too far. You can get to the point where you have spent so long engaging in child-induced conversations about subjects that have no connection to the real world that you start feeling like you have spent your whole life playing *Trivial Pursuit.*

"Emily's little sister eats Play-Doh," Becky reported to me one day, as if it were the most meaningful statement of the decade.

"Well, I think I'll let Emily's mother worry about that one," I replied.

"Emily told her it would turn her face the color of the Play-Doh, but Emily's mother told her she didn't have to worry about that because it would kill her first."

"I just might call Emily's mother and see if scare tactics work for her," I said.

"They don't," Becky answered. "She told us eating ants would make us have nightmares about picnic monsters, but it didn't."

* * *

"Do I have enough money for two doughnuts?" one of Becky's friends asked me one morning at church.

"Yes dear, you have more than enough," I answered, seeing that she had a dollar bill.

When the child started to tear the dollar bill in two so she could pay for the doughnuts with half of it, I showed her, with the patience of a mother who has already made it through toilet training, the proper way to put the dollar in the basket and take fifty cents back. That is when another little girl walked up and asked me if she could take fifty cents out of the basket, too. When I told her she could not because she didn't have a dollar, she started to cry; and she ran off to ask her mother why the minister's wife is the only one allowed to take money out of the offering plate.

Pretty soon it all starts sounding alike—and then the danger signs slowly appear. You start humming "Mary Had a Little Lamb" at work; and you automatically turn your head whenever any kid, regardless of age, appearance, or nationality, calls out for "Mommy." One of my friends, who was tied down at home with three toddlers, once excused herself from a church board meeting saying she had to "go to the potty."

While men are looking for ways to add more child-care time into their lives, some women are looking for ways to subtract a little of it. Both are involved in the same search, the search for balance in life, the search for a lifestyle that is marked by both family involvement and personal growth.

Most people insist that neither careers nor children, in themselves, are capable of giving anyone emotional fulfillment. They say, rather, that emotional fulfillment must come from within. People who have trouble finding this fulfillment often take this as a sign that it is time to make some changes in their lives. Maybe they need to enrich their friendships or pursue more outside interests, they reason. Or maybe they need to spend more time with their families or carve out some private time to use to talk to God more often.

One of my friends had allowed herself to get immersed in her children, and she was finding it increasingly difficult to hold onto any measure of self-esteem, especially since all of her actions had to be filtered through her grade schooler's one-word vocabulary: "Yuk!" Eventually, she decided to get out of the house and become more involved in church work. It sounds like a small change, but it made all the difference in the world to her.

"I couldn't believe how totally that little decision changed my outlook on life," she recently told me. "It was as if I had been cured of some horrible disease, as if I were shouting to myself, over and over, 'You really do have a brain after all.' " Then she added, "I found out I could even speak to large groups of people—and they would listen!" This woman had been suffering from a common malady, something like cabin fever, more like playhouse fever. She found her own cure, though, by exercising one of life's many options.

Other women have felt the need to exercise different options. Like my friend Jeannine, for example. She was absolutely sure she would continue working as a nurse after her children were born. That is, until the morning when she came home from her job on the night shift, collapsed on the bed, and was awakened some time later by a knock at the door—it was a neighbor holding her two-year-old and explaining, in a stern voice, "I didn't think you'd want your son wandering around barefoot in the snow all morning with a Pepsi bottle in one hand and a diaper in the other."

After that, Jeannine decided to quit working and stay home with the children. But she didn't bury the career side of her life in the bottom of a diaper pail. Instead, she worked in a volunteer capacity for various medical programs in the city when her children were young. And then, when her youngest was in high school, she began taking the refresher courses that prepared her for her eventual return to full-time work.

Some of the other women I know were able to work full time while their children were small and were able to remain happy and well organized in spite of their extra busy schedules. But these women made their trade-offs, too. Several of them learned to live in unkempt houses, for instance; and others missed the soccer games where their children were named Most Valuable Players—or the grade-school Olympic contests where their children won relay races (by crawling around on the floor pushing dried beans with their faces, making red marks on the same noses that Mother and Father will someday pay a dermatologist three times their salaries to remove red marks from).

The women who choose to put their careers on hold during their children's growing-up years have to learn how to cope with the ego-deflating fact that they do not get paid for their work. They have to accept the fact that they are also losing valuable years outside the job market. One such woman made her decision to "retire" only after returning to work and retaining such a strong desire to have a tidy home, neatly scrubbed kids, and home-cooked, gourmet meals that she found herself rushing home during her work breaks to do household chores.

Years later, this same woman was sitting at her dining room table stringing beans and talking to herself. . . . "What have you done with your life?" she asked herself. "Who are you, really?" And that is when she began to snap out of it. "Come on, girl," she heard herself saying, "you have raised five children. You have done important work in the church and begun some worthwhile programs in the community—programs that are still generating money for good causes. . . ." Soon this woman was planning her future, channeling her talents into some part-time work, and restoring the balance once again.

This is the way life is for most of us. There are choices to exercise all along the way. Sometimes we have to go slow, take our time, try something on a part-time basis before we decide if we truly want to expand our educational goals or choose new career directions. Sometimes it is easy and the road seems clear. Other times we have to stumble through a haze to get anywhere— and life seems pretty scary. "But never let the fear of failure stop you from finding your way in life," one woman warned. "Rather, think of failure as a learning experience—an opportunity to try again toward the successful goal."

And the Search Continues

All parents, both mothers and fathers, eventually find themselves face to face with the same questions: What do you really want out of life? What are your true goals? How are you going to go about taking control? How are you going to get out there and get what you want and still remain true to your spouse, your children, yourself, and your God?

The world is full of choices. And the best advice I have ever heard about how to make them came in the form of a challenge I once received from a good friend. "Think seriously about what gives you the greatest joy in life," she told me, "and then build on that. Perhaps you can work it into a hobby, or an occupation, or a family activity; but build it into your life wherever possible, as fully as possible, as often as possible. For, when you have found the thing that gives you joy, you have found what you were truly created to do."

Parting Tips

When you are concerned with personal growth . . .

—If you are spending too much time with kids, make arrangements to go somewhere alone once in a while—just to see what it feels like to arrive at a destination without having once answered the question, "Are we there yet?"

—If you are missing out on home and hearth, set aside some time to spend in one-on-one activities with your children. The activities have to be fun though. Cleaning out the mold that is growing in a child's closet doesn't count.

—Accept the fact that both children and adults need their own "space." I once rushed outside like a mad woman to see why my "baby" was crying, only to find out that she was playing house with some neighbor children; and she was playing the part of the infant.

—Never confuse spending time taking care of the house with spending time with the kids. "I spent enough time acting on my perfectionist housekeeping tendencies to have gone around the world four times," one mother admitted, "but then I found out that compulsively neat women are nothing more than a pain in the tail to their spouses and children."

—Think about the future. Ask yourself where you want to be ten years from now, what kind of person you want to have become by then, and whether or not this fits in with your growing understanding of God's plan for your life.

13

Is There Romance after Children?

The Husband-Wife Relationship

". . . for a prostitute can be had for the price of a loaf, but a married woman is out for bigger game."

— Proverbs 6:26, NEB

—"How in the world can anyone feel like slipping into something sexy when four chocolate-coated five-year-olds are in the next room showing each other their bottoms?"

—"I'm beginning to believe it is totally impossible to keep a passionate marriage relationship alive and well in between soccer games."

—"Since I became a parent, the time for sex with my spouse is pretty much limited to the time we have left after we finally get the kids to bed—and you can tell, by the way I say the word *finally,* that there is very little energy left after that."

Sound familiar? From fettuccine and candlelight to pasta that is shaped like cute little ABCs and a light that is bright enough to reveal whether or not the green peas are being eaten or slipped under the table. No matter how you look at it, nothing can kill a torrid romance quicker than sharing your life with a third person who is a crack shot with a water pistol.

Did True Love Ever Really Conquer All?

Revis and I celebrated our seventeenth wedding anniversary at a very expensive restaurant last year. We had almost forgotten

151

what it was like to order from a menu that doesn't have zoo animals running up and down its edges. Needless to say, we were ecstatic.

During the evening, the restaurant hostess seated a young couple at a table near us. They were out for the evening with their parents—a fact which did nothing whatsoever to cramp their style. For, right in the middle of this elegant restaurant, the young couple proceeded to feed each other an entire five-course dinner; from shrimp cocktail to chocolate mousse, they held spoons, forks, and cups to each other's mouths. They didn't take turns either. Not once. Instead, their utensils moved together, at the same time, perfectly synchronized; and the couple were even able to caress each other's arms while they were performing this feat. *Is there a class in this somewhere?* I began to wonder. I could just see what would have happened if Revis and I had tried anything like that. We would have ended up looking like a two-year-old looks at the end of each meal.

"Do you suppose they've been married for seventeen years?" I whispered to my husband.

"Not even seventeen days," he whispered back.

He was probably right. At least one thing is for sure. That couple doesn't have any children. Lifting a spoon to another person's mouth could not seem nearly that romantic to someone who is going to spend the following morning trying to stuff spoonfuls of mushy oatmeal into a mouth that thrives on spitting them back at him.

According to a recent Ann Landers survey, 70 percent of today's parents would choose not to have children if they had it to do over again. It would not surprise me to find out that a number of those people answered that question the day after yet another thwarted night spent tending to nightmares and stomachaches instead of to sex.

Divorce is common in the early years of marriage, probably at least in part because so many new parents can't find a successful way to deal with the new demands on their time and energy. They aren't comfortable with their new roles; they aren't sure they can relate to each other as Mom and Dad and still get excited about relating to each other as friend or lover. And they don't know how to work the children into all of it. "Even when our bedroom door is locked," one couple confided, "we are worrying about what the kids are getting into out there."

There is no way around it. Parenting is a twenty-four-hour-a-day job. And yet, there are many parents who have learned to adjust to the changes that come from giving birth—parents who say that their marriages are better than ever.

Information, Please

A number of couples have very unrealistic expectations of what is involved when children are brought into a marriage. They've never before had anyone interrupt their kisses with stories about stuffed dinosaurs or serenade their private discussions with music from a bunch of homemade instruments that even Mister Rogers would be hard pressed to praise. This is probably why it is so easy to make mistakes.

"I put my kids first in my life," one woman told me, "although I knew that my husband resented this terribly." It is an easy trap to fall into: living for our children, forgetting that those children are only loaned to us for eighteen or so years, while our marriage relationships are meant to last for life—long after the last child has gone out the door with his Bruce Springsteen posters and Foreigner tapes (and just about everything else except his dirty laundry).

During a business trip with Revis, I once found myself sitting in a restaurant with a woman who suddenly started to cry. She caught me completely off guard. For, we had only been talking about the price of pot roast. I can see where that might make a nervous cow or two cry, but this seemed a little ridiculous.

"Oh, never mind me," the woman explained, motioning toward a family who had just been seated at a table across the room. "Every time I see a little boy, I break down and cry."

Assuming this woman had lost a son, I tried to be extra understanding. "I guess it really must be hard for you," I agreed sympathetically.

"It sure is," the woman replied. "I've been away from my own little boy for almost forty-eight hours now, and I feel so empty when he's not with me."

At first, I started chastising myself, wondering what kind of wicked mother I must be. Thinking of my own two days away from my child as nothing less than the luxury trip of a lifetime, with no juice to wipe up and no Pudding Pops to split precisely down the middle under threat of being slapped with a maternal malpractice suit by Becky and her friends. True, I missed my daughter, and things certainly seemed different without her; but I had been thinking of my short time apart from Becky and my time alone with Revis as a pretty great experience for all three of us.

"That's what it is," I told myself. "She's all alone on this trip, and she's just not used to that."

"Maybe it would be different if your husband were with you," I tried to console her.

"He is," she grimaced. "That's the worst part."

I didn't feel so guilty after that. Only thankful that I was still working at making my marriage a priority in my life, and that my husband and I could get away together once in a while and actually enjoy ourselves, and that we had done this often enough to know that our child was secure and happy in our absence. Yes, the marriage relationship can still be fun. Even after you have figured out that parenting involves a lot of sleepless (for the wrong reasons) nights.

Revis and I don't always have loads of fun with our marriage, of course. Sometimes we get out of the habit of going on dates, even though we know you can eat hot dogs and go to Disney movies only so long before you start talking like a kindergarten teacher. (Once I went out to dinner with Revis after having eaten in fast-food restaurants so often that, when the waiter asked me how I would like my meat, I thought he wanted me to choose between broiled and fried.)

Other times, we forget that couple time alone together doesn't just happen, and we stop planning any for a while. Once I even allowed myself to become naive enough to believe that a family vacation would fill the need for couple-together time.

Family vacations are asexual. Thus, it is useless to include them in any of your romantic plans. It doesn't help to take Grandma along either. I tried that one year so Revis and I could have a private motel room; but when Becky wasn't knocking at the door with important messages about the hours the pool would be open, Grandma was calling on the phone to tell us she wasn't sure Becky should go to the pool on such a windy day. I read somewhere that more people seek help from their psychiatrists right after their summer vacations than at any other time. I am not the least bit surprised.

How to Keep the Home Fires Burning

The couples I know who have managed to keep the home fires burning (in their bedrooms, that is) while they are raising their children have chosen to put large amounts of time and energy into their marriages. They believe that the lasting kind of love between a man and a woman is dependent upon an act of the will, not upon a random shot from Cupid's bow. And they also believe it takes a lot more "will" to build a good marriage when you have to build it during coffee breaks from Junior Scrabble games. Therefore, such couples work at marriage; and they are well aware of the potential danger signs.

One marriage counselor, interviewed in a newspaper article, cited several signs that point toward marital trouble. These ranged from boredom to financial problems to terminally messy garages (the latter being a sign that the couple cannot cooperate well enough to clean it up). I don't think this means that every couple whose garage looks like mine should start digging out their pre-nuptial agreements, but it probably does mean that you can tell a lot about a couple by noticing the little things in their lives.

I once heard a speaker insist that mates who kiss good-bye in the morning live $5\frac{1}{2}$ years longer and make 20 to 30 percent more money. I'm not sure where he got his statistics, but there is no doubt in my mind that life's small gestures are critically important. Of course, in order to show love for one's spouse in little ways, one has to spend time with that spouse.

Most couples have to work hard at carving out together-time from their busy schedules. One such couple finally found out that the only way they could have a sizable chunk of time to talk to each other every day was to do the dishes together. "Just announce that you are going to do dishes, and you won't see any of your kids for at least two hours," they explained. Eventually, this couple bought a dishwasher, and they insist it almost ruined their marriage.

Couples who have a weekday off from work frequently use this time, when the children are safely tucked away at their school desks, to go out to breakfast and spend a few stolen hours together. Other couples are able to ease their children into an early enough bedtime to spend their wide awake evening hours with each other. This works sometimes, but not always. One couple who worked hard to arrange their daily schedule this way were forced back to square one when Grandmother moved in with them. "She actually used to come in and tuck us into bed at night," the couple groaned. "We would drop hints by saying, 'Is there anything we can do for you, Mother?' But to no avail."

Many people have told me that the key to keeping a marriage exciting is found in a couple's sense of appreciation for each other. Once, at a Christian family retreat, the couples present were asked to list ten things they like about their spouses; and then they were instructed to pray for those spouses. It was an eye-opening experience for many people, including me. For, I already knew I didn't like my mate's habit of eating three-fourths of the pizza; but I had forgotten how sexy he really looks in that tweed suit I bought him last Christmas. The fewer of those kinds of things we forget, the greater will be our capacity for having fun together.

How to Make the Home Fires Sizzle

A short time ago, *Ladies' Home Journal* magazine surveyed 83,000 wives who described themselves as sexually satisfied. These women were asked to share some of their tips, and they did. They advised, among other things, trading off reading and TV time for sex, improving your body and your self-image, and making a deal with yourself never to worry about the day's stresses after the bedroom door is closed. I couldn't agree more. In our house, however, when the bedroom door is closed, it doesn't always remain closed. Example . . .

Saturday morning, 9:00 A.M. Becky bangs on our bedroom door hard enough to convince us she has just broken at least two bones in her body. We jump for cover, rearrange the blankets, try to regain a breathing pattern normal enough to appear as if we have just spent the last half hour leisurely thumbing through *Newsweek* magazine. As it turns out, Becky's bones are fully workable, and she has come to our room because she can't re-

member if the "Smurfs" are on channel two or channel five;
and she is too lazy to look in the *TV Guide.*

"You're all sweaty, Mom and Dad," she gasps, feeling our
foreheads. "I'd better get the thermometer and take your tempera-
tures."

It doesn't always help to wait until midnight either. Once, right
in the middle of the night, our play time was interrupted by a
frantic knock on the bedroom door.

"I woke up, and I couldn't go back to sleep," Becky informed us.

"Why?" Revis asked, with as much parental concern as can
be mustered by someone who doesn't know where his pajamas
are.

"I got to thinking I don't know how many buttonholes I
own, and I thought maybe I'd better count them before I forget
about it."

Other parents have similar stories to tell. "Our kids go to bed
so late we'd have to have sex three hours after David Letterman
has gone to bed if we wanted to do it at night," one mother
remarked.

"When the children were little, Bill always came home tired
from work, but the kids weren't nearly as tired from school,"
another mother commented, "so I literally had to wake him up
at night or we'd probably have remained celibate for the entire
twenty-five years our children were at home."

She is only one of a number of women who admit that their
sex lives were not nearly as steamy as they might have liked
while the children were growing up.

When the Fire Needs to Be Rekindled

Many couples trade baby-sitting duties with friends so they
can send their children to someone else's house overnight or
for a weekend once in a while. Others take long, leisurely baths
together after their children are in bed and find that they have
more energy left over than they thought they did. (Remember,
this is not the time to share new ideas you have heard on potty
training.)

Such couples try to remind themselves, often, that they are

husband and wife, not just mother and father. They believe you can even help your children feel more secure when you model for them a strong, romantic bond. I didn't realize how true this is until the day my daughter asked me a very significant question.

"Why do you always call him Daddy?" she inquired, motioning toward her father.

"I call him Revis sometimes," I replied a bit too defensively.

"Only when you are mad at him."

Married couples need to work at nurturing their primary relationship with each other, one to one, in trust and love. Most of us are well aware of this, just as we are well aware of how difficult it can sometimes be to build this kind of relationship. This is why so many couples talk about the importance of total fidelity throughout married life, even when the children are still tumbling through the house, even when you are tempted to believe the old myth about the grass being greener in someone else's waterbed.

I once saw a movie in which one of the characters was comparing faithfulness in marriage to a teapot. The character said it is very important to keep your teapot intact, because if you break it and then glue it back together, it could shatter into a million pieces years later. This sounded like such a perfect analogy to me, so I made the mistake of sharing it with my husband, knowing full well that he doesn't get nearly as enthusiastic about perfect analogies as I do.

"What do you think about teapots?" I asked at the end of my monologue."

"Is this a trick question?" Revis mumbled in much the same tone of voice Becky once used to tell me she doesn't think I should expect her to go to bed as early as her friend Allyson does because Allyson has blonde hair.

Still, I think we all realize the importance of keeping the loving, faithful marriage bond strong and secure. And, with a little extra effort, this is not impossible to do, even for those who find themselves in the position of being both spouse and parent. In fact, according to some medical research, couples who have given birth to children actually tend to have more sexual confidence, more sensuality, and more pride in their bodies than people who haven't. This is often attributed to the fact that a couple is likely to feel more intimacy and commitment within their marriage relationship after having shared the birth experience. They are also likely to be more sexually playful, having learned during the pregnancy that playfulness is a crucial element involved in trying to work around an abdomen that would fit so perfectly into a Santa Claus costume.

People who become parents are also likely to mature during the process, and this isn't necessarily bad for a sexual relationship. True, it is a bit removed from the first youthful blush of romance, the kind of chemistry that makes you alternate between shivers and cold sweats (sort of like coming down with the flu, except you don't feel that your life is over when the flu goes away); but many people insist that this initial attraction can grow into something even better if it is properly nurtured.

"Marital intimacy grows much deeper as the couple builds their spiritual bond together," a minister told me. That is why it is so important for husbands and wives to read the Bible together and pray together and actively share religious experiences together. One counselor I know even advises young couples not to spend a lot of time in prayer together until they are married. He feels that the spiritual bond can draw a couple so intimately together that sex is the logical next step.

Certainly, there is something to be said for the mystical blend of marriage and faith and the act of two people becoming one under God. For God planned it to be that way, and He surely expects us to work at keeping our marriages healthy and viable. Even secular research studies speak strongly to this issue. *Redbook* magazine, in fact, published survey responses concerning the sexual pleasures of 100,000 American women and concluded that the religious female is the most sexually satisfied and the most orgasmic woman in the country.

"I guess it merely proves that you can't practice either religion or sex just on Christmas and Easter and expect to have much success at either one," I joked to a friend when we were discussing the article. But I am well aware that the issue is more complex than that.

According to the research compiled by *Redbook,* religious women usually feel better about themselves and about their world, thus enhancing their sexual pleasure. Survey responses also reflect the fact that Christian circles give a lot of attention to marriage enrichment and the fact that both sex and religion involve "letting yourself go." The article concluded with these words: "Religion at its best is a way of bringing together those things that make for sex at its best—commitment, mutual respect, shared values, meaningful intimacy. And those are the things that make the earth move."[9] I can't think of any way to say it better.

Parting Tips

When it is time for romance . . .

—Never give up the fine art of dating just because you get married. You may not feel goose bumps every time you hold hands in the movie theater anymore, but look on the bright side. At least you can enjoy your cheeseburger without having to work around that knot in your stomach—and you can go home to bed together at the end of the evening.

—Be yourself. Tell each other how you feel and what you want. "I always felt guilty about being aggressive in the bedroom," said one wife and mother, "but that was before I asked my husband what he thought about it."

—Be flexible. True, maybe you are no longer able to find enough privacy to lie in the middle of the living room floor and make love; but, if you listen to your children long enough, they will convince you that you are getting to the age when it would probably just give you a backache anyway.

—Learn to lock your bedroom door. I much prefer this to the fairly widespread practice of putting Vaseline on the doorknob. (One of my friends started locking her door only after her daughter's seven-year-old overnight guest walked into the master bedroom at 2:00 A.M. and woke up the entire neighborhood screaming that a vampire was in the house biting a lady's neck.)

—Spend enough time together and enough time with your God to make your marriage what you want it to be. It is the only way for any couple to avoid moving through life in opposite directions.

14

When You'd Rather Punt
Those Moments Parents Dread Most

"Trust in the Lord with all your heart. Never rely on what you think you know."
—Proverbs 3:5, TEV

The moments parents dread most. You know what they are, whether you have experienced them or not. The messy room showdown, when you notice your child's room is littered with old candy wrappers from companies that have since gone out of business . . . the day when the neighborhood kids decide that you live in the best house on the street and reward you for this great feat by planning the six-year-old equivalent of a block party at your home . . . the day when your child starts learning how to memorize phone numbers, and you catch him calling for an ambulance to take G.I. Joe to the hospital . . . and, perhaps the most fearsome moment of all, the day when you happen to see your child's elementary school sign-out sheet and discover that every self-respecting kid over the age of five visits an orthodontist at least once a month.

The list could go on and on. But let's zero in on a few of the moments and see if we can learn anything from them. Take, for example, dental appointments, parties, and child photography.

Teeth, Teeth, and More Teeth

I remember the first time Becky ever asked me about the word *orthodontist.* She didn't pronounce it right because she had heard it from some kids at school who were talking through their braces. "Are orthodontists nice to children, Mommy?" she wanted to know.

"Yes dear, they are very nice to children," I told her, "because the children's parents pay them a lot of money to be nice."

The subject of teeth is an important topic of conversation in a home where children reside. Almost from the moment of the child's birth, in fact, you find yourself spending a lot of time thinking about teeth—cutting them, brushing them, pulling them. Soon, you discover that the other people who inhabit your child's world are interested in teeth, too.

Last year, I got a call from Becky's school principal. He said I'd better get right over to the school because my child had been hit in the mouth in gym class, and two of her teeth had been knocked down into her gums. I dumped the meringue I was making down the garbage disposal (meringue waits for nothing, not even tooth trouble) and rushed crazily out of the house, having to make two trips back inside for car keys. By the time I began my panicky drive to school, I was the true embodiment of motherhood, looking like I had just stepped out of a punk rock beauty shop.

It wasn't until I had arrived at the school and checked my daughter's mouth (which was, by that time, back to its normal state—lots of talk) that I realized the two teeth the principal thought had been knocked down into the gum were new permanent teeth that hadn't even come in yet.

Other parents have similar tooth stories to tell. Like the mother whose daughter accidentally flushed two retainers down the toilet; or the father who tied his son's tooth to the door and ended up breaking the door and not budging the tooth.

You spend a lot of time at the dentist's office after you become a parent. And, if you have always been the type who would rather get called up for an IRS audit than get your teeth cleaned, this can be somewhat traumatic. "The first filling is always the hardest," Becky's dentist told me when he found a pinpoint cavity in a baby tooth. Then he added with a smile, "On the parents, I mean."

He was right, of course. Becky came through the whole thing without a whimper. I was banished to the waiting room, which I figured was the place reserved for bad little parents. The nurse told me it was routine procedure, designed to allow me to pace the floor in solitude (which, translated, means "out of the dentist's hair").

When my daughter came out of the office that day, weighted down with "good little girl" stickers and the other kinds of sugarless goodies stocked by today's enlightened dentists, she was babbling, "When do I get my saliva back, Doctor?" (She had been told a little machine would take away her saliva while the dentist did his work.)

"They always do this well until they get old enough to start hearing stories from other kids at school," the nurse informed me as I cheerfully paid her more than it cost my mother to raise me to age eighteen. "We had one little boy in here last week who was scared to death because his friend had told him the dentist uses a Black & Decker drill."

Obviously, the key to all of this would have to be found in remaining calm and trusting the people around you to do their jobs correctly—and being able to sit in a dental office waiting room and read *People* magazines while you pray that your child's teeth are coming in straight.

Party Time Blues

The very mention of the word *party* can bring untold excitement to the eyes of a grade-school child, and wreak havoc in the minds of his mother and father. I was initiated into the parent party club (you pay your dues as you go—and pay and pay and pay) with what I had assumed would be the first of many simple little birthday parties for Becky. But I had forgotten that nothing remains simple when one or more children are involved.

Before long, I was having big birthday parties for Becky on the front lawn. Each year, the guest list continued to grow until, by the third time around, all of my friends had become strangely unavailable to help out on that particular day.

Some people say that the number of children at a child's birthday party should equal the child's age in years, but I never figured out how you could choose a handful of children from those long lists of "best friends." What criteria could you use? IQ? Number of freckles? Behavior? (I was tempted.)

I did decide to set an age limit one year, however; and I put a time limit on the party, too. Otherwise, I might have ended up with a longer guest list than the one I used for my wedding— and I might also have been stuck with the kids for the weekend. (Parents of young children can easily get carried away when they are given an unlimited amount of free time.)

No matter what limits I used, though, there always seemed to be large numbers of people at every one of Becky's birthday parties. One year the total number really did get out of hand. Thank goodness one of the mothers bailed me out by volunteering to take the older children to the park.

"Betsy, are you sure?" I said.

"Sure I'm sure," she laughed. "Remember I'm the one who leads the junior highs at church. I guess I'm just a self-destructive person at heart." And I began to breathe again.

I finally decided I was trying too hard. I was remembering the birthday parties of my own childhood, when all the mothers would stage elaborate theme parties with twelve wading pools set up in a backyard and buried treasures hidden in sandboxes. One of those mothers had even concocted a petting zoo for her son's birthday party. But she didn't have a career to worry with or a van full of kids to drive to the regional science fair the following day.

I know one mother who used to host a picnic for her child's entire class on the last day of school each year. She always served hot dogs and pop and ice cream bars (we weren't into health food back then), and the children would cry when they had to go home—a sure sign of success to any mother who has had experience on the children's party circuit.

Another mother told me she didn't want to think about the elegant pink-laced birthday parties she used to plan for her little girl, but she insists that they did teach her an important lesson in life. "The little girls wore dresses most of the time back then, so they would come to the party in their normal attire," she pointed out, "but the little boys whose everyday clothes were overalls would come dressed up like little gentlemen." And, while the girls threw spitballs and hid plastic spiders in the cake icing, the boys behaved perfectly. "The way you dress them determines the way they act," this mother contends.

There are other people who agree with this assessment. A junior high home economics teacher, for example, still remembers the first day her students were allowed to wear jeans to class—and the problems she had trying to keep them from sitting on the kitchen counters.

Of course, not everyone would agree that party dress makes the child, but most of us would love to find a way to get through our children's birthday parties in one piece. I have one friend who used to bake a special cake for the birthday child in her family and allow him to sit in the "King Chair" (the dining-room chair with arms on it) during a family dinner. The family called this a birthday party. But that was years ago. I figure most of today's parents could duplicate something like this only if they have children who have never discussed birthday parties with anyone under the age of twelve. Unfortunately, however, such children, as far as I can tell, are no longer being born.

"At the very least," one friend warned me, "remember that you have to decide exactly when you are going to bring your children into the world if you are planning to have birthday parties for them." She told me to have my kids between June 1 and September 1 or not have them at all.

"Don't spend a lot of time planning complicated games either," another mother remarked. "Most young children can entertain themselves very well at parties simply by making mustaches out of the ice cream or by falling down and getting grass stains on their clothes and thinking it is hysterical."

I have one more idea to add to those. I saw it in a cartoon. An already harassed-looking mother informed the children as they arrived at her son's birthday party that the first one to leave would get a special present.

Then there are the other kinds of parties, like slumber parties, for instance. I decided to start easing Becky into this inescapable phenomenon of childhood by allowing her to have only one over-night guest at a time. But the first time we tried this, my daughter ended up in our bedroom at midnight crying her eyes out because her friend had gone to sleep first.

Many mothers have advised me to plan plenty of activities

for large slumber parties and to get the opinions of several guests rather than rely on my own opinion of what I think the children might like to do. "At the slumber parties at my house, you will find some kids playing Monopoly and others baking cookies," one mother explained, "but I figure if they are busy, they aren't as likely to come up with the idea of rigging up a booby trap bucket of water over the bathroom door or staging a pizza eating contest in the middle of the street.

My friend Judy almost gave up on slumber parties. It happened the night her little girl's sleep-over friend was "not very hungry" for dinner, that is, not until the two friends had come back to the house after a ball game. Judy found the girls in the kitchen eating candy, peanuts, potato chips, and onion dip. "When they ran out of dip, they licked the bowl," she cringed, "and when they started rummaging through the refrigerator looking for dill pickles, I announced that it was time to go to bed." Needless to say, the overnight friend soon developed such a bad tummyache that her mother had to come and take her home at 1:00 A.M. Merely one more reminder to those of us who are parents to hold fast to the only parental motto that applies in every stage of parenting: "This too shall pass."

The Picture That Is Worth Nowhere Near a Thousand Words

A beautiful color portrait of your child for only eighty-two cents. Who can resist? I can. And, left alone, I could have gone on resisting forever. . . . "But Mother," I kept saying, "we have all those home movies and slides and really good snapshots." Still, it was no use. I was trying to reason with a woman who once bought a fireplace screen "because it looked so pretty in the ad," in spite of the fact that she had no fireplace. That kind of woman is not about to be the only grandmother in the world without an eighty-two-cent special.

"Everybody else is doing it," Mother said.

"I think I used that argument on you a few times in past years," I replied, "and you always told me that I wasn't everybody."

My mother ignored my reply. Then she thrust an ad into my hand and explained how guilty I would feel if I forced her to muddle through her sunset years without that eighty-two-cent color portrait of her only grandchild. Besides, it was almost Christmas; and I really wanted that new pair of earrings Mother had been hinting she might buy me.

Most of my friends thought I gave in too easily. One of them told me that a child photographer once asked her to imagine how bad she would feel if her son got run over by a car and left her without a good color portrait. Another friend said a child photographer gave her a sob story about a woman who refused to buy pictures and then went home to find her husband having a heart attack. "If you do decide to buy pictures," this woman suggested, "be sure to read the fine print so you won't end up having to buy three dozen pictures of your child with her tongue stuck out."

A third friend was sure I would have trouble making it past the waiting line, where all those children are being "tortured" by their own parents in the name of photography. . . . "You're going to sit there and look happy if I have to paddle you all day," one mother screams at her son, while the one behind her tries a different approach. "But you're such a darling little girl," she coos, "and this is how Wonder Woman got her start." Having heard all this, I figured that, at the very least, I was fully prepared for my own personal venture into the fun house known as the child photography studio.

I finally got up my nerve and dialed the number of one of the stores advertising a photo special. I politely asked how many pictures a person is required to buy in the eighty-two cent photo promotion, and was told, by someone who sounded like she was a trainee on loan from the Sleazy Bar and Grill, "I dunno."

Then, the night before our appointment, Becky slept on her hair wrong and had to have it washed, an experience she ranks about two points below getting a booster shot. "You'll love getting your picture taken," I rambled on, trying to keep her from crying into the no-tears shampoo. "The photographer will have toys for you to see." But she was only mildly impressed, probably sensing that she was not going to get something for nothing.

When we arrived at the store, the photographer asked me to choose a background: "We have woodsy, cloudy . . ."

"Do you have murky?" I asked. He didn't smile.

We spent the first few minutes trying to make Becky laugh, but we eventually switched tactics and decided to settle for getting her to sit up straight on the bench. She was afraid of falling, she said, so the photographer proceeded to tell her that she would, indeed, fall if she didn't obey all of his instructions. I scowled at him, and he snapped four pictures of my daughter looking like she was sitting in front of a firing squad.

"How could he?" I groaned to myself. I had given him the chance to photograph the most beautiful child in the world, and he had blown it.

"Come back in three weeks," he said. "I know these pictures will make your Christmas holiday a happy one."

"Ho ho ho," I mumbled.

For the next few days, I cried on friends' shoulders. The ones who had several children helped me the most. "Don't let it bother you," one consoled. "Pictures seem too important with the first child. By the time we had our fourth, we had sold our camera." And yet, I still continued to cringe at the thought of going back to that store and looking at the finished product in living color.

When I finally did, the salesclerk began preparing me for the worst. "Remember the pictures where the photographer told your little girl not to smile?" she asked.

"He never got the chance," I answered dryly.

As it turned out, I was allowed to choose between two photographs (the lessers of all the other evils), but, for only $79.95, I could have a number of additional pictures of my child crying. I sighed. The child herself sat at my side looking very noncommittal. I soon found my mind wandering toward the people in the other booths.

"At least they were lucky," I mused, but when I finally exited with my eighty-two cent booby prize, I got the chance to glance at a couple of the pictures the other mothers were "oohing and aahing" over. I was amazed. "True love, among mothers, actually is blind," I concluded.

"Maybe next Christmas," the check-out lady smiled, "or try us in the spring. It could have been the backdrop."

"I know those photographers have to make a living," I said, "and I know that some of their portraits really are good and some of their customers really are happy, but . . ."

"Eighty-two cents, please," she replied.

I handed her the change and ushered Becky out the door. "Your grandmother is going to pay for this one," I grumbled on the way to the car. "Oh, boy, is your grandmother going to pay for this one."

I had, once again, lost my all important parental cool.

Whose Idea Was It to Have Kids Anyway?

There are many ways to cope with parenthood's most dreaded moments. Really there are. It's just that, once you get the hot chocolate cleaned off the ceiling, few of them seem worth the effort.

"Try to remember what it felt like to be seven years old," a friend suggested when Becky interrupted my first lecture as a full-fledged author with a loud rendition of "Home on the range, where the deer and the envelope play." And I do remember some of it. Mostly though, I remember my parents being able to silence me anytime, anywhere, with little more than a secret family wink. The trouble is, I never learned how to wink.

Many people tell me it helps to keep a positive outlook on life while you are attempting to deal with the trials and tribulations of parenthood. They also say it helps not to take everything so seriously. These people are undoubtedly right. I once read that 98 percent of the things we worry about never happen. My first reaction? "But what about the other 2 percent?" And then I caught myself. "I have to think positive. I have to remember that each stage in a child's life contains both good and bad; and, however much you have to strain to do it, you must find the good things and emphasize them."

If all else fails, I finally decided, I'm just going to try to hang on to one of Murphy's most graphic laws: "Eat one live toad the first thing in the morning and nothing worse will happen to you the rest of the day." And then it hit me. Even when I am down, even when I am sure I can't handle the difficult moments of parenting, all is not lost. I can always grab hold of those moments and use them as insurance whenever I sense those familiar old feelings creeping up on me—and telling me this might be a good time to start thinking about having another baby.

Parting Tips

When you are faced with the kinds of moments parents dread . . .

—Keep your expectations realistic. Expect your child's ballet school to elect you to sew 250 costumes for the dance recital. Then you will be pleasantly surprised when you are handed only twenty yards of nondescript net and told to make a French poodle out of it.

—Make it clear to your children that there are certain words and phrases they must never use—like, "My mom and dad will do it."

—Let your feelings out once in a while. According to Carol Eisen Rinzler, writing for *Woman's Day* magazine, "Parents who yell now and then rarely spend their sunset years in the looney bin."

—Don't hesitate to get family counseling if your problems seem impossible to solve. If things aren't that bad, however, you can try talking with your friends. When it comes to parenting, misery truly does love company.

—Turn to God often during these days. He, too, is a parent—and He has "been there" with each one of us.

15

Things I Said I Would Never Do As a Parent . . .

And a Few Conclusions

". . . even a fool may be thought wise and intelligent if he stays quiet and keeps his mouth shut."
                                                    —Proverbs 17:28, TEV

As you have probably surmised by now, before I became a parent, I wasn't sure I would be a good one. However, I was sure of one thing. I was sure there were certain things I would never do once the label *parent* was added to my portfolio. Here are a few of those.

I would never talk like my mother. I promised myself I would never use those tired old expressions that my mother used so often—expressions like "eat all your vegetables because there are starving children in the world" and "always wear clean under-wear because you never know when you might be in a wreck." I knew better than to ever say things like that to my kid. But then, one day, I caught myself telling Becky to "Stop crying, or I'll give you something to cry about," and I knew I was trapped.

These days, I sometimes even find myself repeating the worst possible clichés from my childhood, but using different words to say them. Last week, for example, when Becky ranted and raved about my not letting her go out of town with a kid whose parents are bound to make it into the newspaper "police briefs" any day now.

"Why can't I?" she kept asking me. "Why?"

"I'm simply pulling rank on you this time," I replied, and then it hit me. "I can't believe it," I admonished myself. "I just said 'because I told you so.' "

I guess most parents do end up repeating things they were told as children. It doesn't seem to be a matter of whether those things are right or wrong either. It's more like . . . if you don't say them, what else are you going to say?

I would never make my children feel guilty. "By the time I was your age," my father used to tell me, "I was working for penny tips at the corner drugstore." I never figured out how that was supposed to make me feel. Was I supposed to be happy he was able to get a job at all in those depression days? Sad that he couldn't play stickball with the other kids after school? Or certain that he must also have walked long distances to school amid tornados and blizzards? I guess the target was really my conscience. At any rate, that was only the beginning of the guilt tactics my parents used.

All through the years these tactics continued. "I don't see how you can listen to that loud stuff and not care that you could be ruining your ears. . . . We didn't raise you to go running off to some movie every time your Aunt Hazel comes to visit." (I would have signed up for an extra course in trigonometry to avoid Aunt Hazel.)

I tried to get by without using such methods with my first child, but I soon found out that guilt is a parent's most effective weapon. I also found out that my parents used it because they loved me so much. And besides, I'm not sure how I will end up if I enter the future not practiced enough to say, "Don't get me anything for my birthday this year." Or, "Go ahead and go; I'll be fine all alone in this crime-infested world." Or, "I understand completely why you don't have time to visit me anymore."

I would never talk to people about my favorite laundry detergent or my pet remedy for diaper rash. Nevertheless, I soon became as boring as any other parent on the block. Maybe I never even had a chance. I've often heard that you can strike up a conversation with someone, and the thing that is weighing most heavily on each person's mind will surface during the conversation in some way in the first few minutes. The bad part about this is that the thing that is usually weighing most heavily on a parent's mind is either dirty laundry or diaper rash.

I used to think that people who sat around talking about life with baby should have been concentrating on the real issues—like war and disease and poverty. But then, after I became a parent, I discovered that life with baby *is* the real issue. The only difference is that war becomes sibling rivalry and disease becomes ear infections and poverty becomes what all of us experience after we have the children.

Thus, I can now sit for hours arguing the merits of girl babies versus boy babies. And, if I have told one person I have told a thousand that Becky, after seeing *West Side Story,* told me she would sing to her husband when he died, but she would wait until he was old—and that Becky's little friend asked for more dog biscuits at dinner when he really wanted hushpuppies.

I would never believe that my kid is better than the kid down the street. But I hadn't counted on giving birth to the most beautiful, intelligent, talented little girl ever to walk the face of the earth. Now, as the story goes, other people's kids have smart mouths while my daughter has a vocabulary that is advanced for her age. Other people's kids are "know-it-alls," while my daughter is a bit more precocious than most.

For years, I've heard the joke that begins with one parent telling a second, "If that were my kid, I'd tan him good," and ends with the second parent answering, "If that were your kid I'd tan him good, too." But somehow I never realized how much cuter the peanut butter could look on your own baby's face.

I would never say, "If only I had known then what I know now." The phrase always sounded so stale to me, and so defeatist. But that was before I had completely grasped the fact that young children can go from being extremely sensitive one minute to being extremely insensitive the next. Like the little boy who tried to get his school teacher out of a lesson plan that was flopping by whispering to his friend, "Quick, ask her about birds or butterflies." On another day, the same child told his teacher, who was visibly losing weight, "You're getting skinny. You aren't straight yet. You're still round, but you're getting skinny." And he thought it was a great compliment.

It took me a while to learn that a parent has to be everything from a business manager to a nutritionist to a tutor to a private-duty nurse—although, I really should have known the part about the nurse. After all, I do have a mother who once fainted in a movie theater when an actress crushed a wineglass in her hand, a mother who instructed me to call Daddy at work instead of ever showing her any injury more extensive than a hangnail. Still, there are a lot of things you forget until you have kids of your own.

Take kid jargon, for example. I don't remember much about that from my childhood, which is probably why it took me so long to realize that very young children think of the words *mother* and *father* as titles, not as relationships. Hence, a friend of Becky's might tell me, "Your father is here" when she sees Revis coming home from work, and I might rush to the phone and set up an appointment for him to have a face-lift or throw the kid out of the house on the grounds of irreconcilable play. All because I didn't know then what I know now.

I would never nag my children about manners. I got so tired of hearing, "Pass me the corn, *what?*" or, "Did you remember to say thank you?" And then there were all those little rhymes: "Martha, Martha, strong and able, keep your elbows off the table." (I always wondered if they ever used that with someone who was really named Martha.)

Before long, however, I found out that you can't take a child anywhere if he has not been taught to keep his food in his own mouth and his hands off anything you can't bounce on a floor. Now I know how to nag with the best of them.

I would never show a lack of understanding for my children. I was so sure my parents never truly understood me. I would beg to be allowed to talk on the phone for three hours, knowing they wouldn't let me. I figured it was because they had never experienced true love of the sort that could only be kept alive with three-hour phone conversations. Or, if they had, they were certainly too old to remember what it felt like.

When my father would inform me, "I know you are doing that because . . ." and then dare to tell me the rationale behind my actions (and get it exactly right), I would be furious. But that was before I had a daughter of my own. That was before I myself had given up trying to understand a ridiculously moody seven-year-old who alternates between having best friends and ex-best friends—or a martyred eight-year-old who uses her bossiness to cover the hurt she feels when her "boy friend" makes a frog face at her.

"There is no way to fully understand," I moan whenever those impossible moments arise. I moan fairly often.

Countdown to Conclusions

Life is different for each of us who wear the title *parent*. Some of us have lots of children. Others have only one. Some of us find that our marriages grow stronger as we face each new crisis of family life. Others find themselves joining the ranks of single parents, who have to raise their children alone. Most of us discover that our parenting years go by faster than we ever dreamed they could.

"Just when you figure out which disposable diaper is best, the kid gets toilet trained," I once heard a speaker explain. And this is the kind of discovery process that goes on and on. Needless to say, being a parent takes an enormous amount of patience—and love.

And so, we are back, once again, to unconditional positive regard, to tossing away the idea that children are putty to be molded, and to accepting the fact that they are, instead, uniquely created human beings who need an atmosphere of support and encouragement in order to develop their potential.

"Why shouldn't a kid cause trouble in a family where he isn't loved unconditionally?" one minister told me. "After all, he is right when he says he didn't ask to be born."

Unconditional love (and freedom) . . . praying for our children and standing beside those children as they grow and become . . . knowing, all the while, that there are risks . . . but also knowing that just about anything worthwhile in life offers no guarantees and that parenting is certainly one of the most worthwhile ventures anyone could ever undertake.

Thus we come to the most important and the most difficult lesson of all: We have to get to the point where we are willing to let our children be themselves and let our God be God, knowing, full well, that we won't always understand either one.

A woman who just sent her last child off to college told me about her oldest son (now away from home) inviting an old high school buddy over for the evening when they were both in town for a visit. "I simply didn't know how to react," this woman admitted, "sitting there watching these two men in three-piece suits talk about old times, especially since it was the first time I had ever seen either one of them without ponytails and dirty jeans." Then she continued, "I had gotten so used to their old images by that time that I was no longer even sure which way I liked them best."

You change. Your children change. You try to savor the good moments and learn from the bad. Sometimes you enjoy your children more than you ever dreamed possible. Other times, you feel lucky simply to have survived the day. You do some things right, some things wrong; and, occasionally, you just stumble along hoping not to make enough mistakes to get kicked out of the "honorable mention" category of parenting. I once heard an old proverb that goes like this: "To stumble is not necessarily to fall, but to go forward faster." If it is true, I think I just might have it made as a parent after all.

Putting Away Childish Things

And then they grow up—and we should not be surprised. There have been telltale signs all along the way.

"Scott said he liked me better than anybody, even better than the boys," Becky exclaimed, "and his Care Bear kissed my Care Bear when I was at Kirk's birthday party last week!"

"I guess David's reached that 'difficult age,' " my friend Bev sighed, "the age when no one at church will agree to teach his class, and everyone starts looking expectantly at me."

"It has gone too fast," you tell yourself, totally forgetting those days when you used to pray for the strength to do just one more load of diapers.

"Remember when I used to kick and scream like a baby trying to get my way?" Becky asked me yesterday.

"Oh, you mean last week?" I teased.

"Mom! You know I'm not like that anymore. I'm all grown up now."

"The jury is still out on that one," I replied, trying to convince myself more than her. Not because my child is right about being all grown up, but because she actually is growing up. Maybe even faster than she truly believes she is.

All I have to do is turn around these days, and the future slips up and catches me off guard. Most of the parents around me know exactly what I mean. You may have gotten away with adding only seven years to your age during the past ten, but your children are wearing all ten of those years proudly—and openly.

"You're writing a book about five to eight-year-old children?" a parent of teen-agers asked me. "You should title it *These are the Easy Years.*" This woman used to think, like most of us, that successfully parenting young children is the most impossible task of all. But that was before her children had reached the mixed-up years, the years when the hormones take over, the years when a child would rather surrender his jeans to the washing machine than admit that he really does want to please his parents.

"If you took movies of your children as babies, movies of the blackmail variety, now is the time to get them out," one mother said of the teen years. And another came up with an even better idea. "These are the years when you should ask yourself if your child has ever shown any interest in visiting a distant relative," she explained, "like in Outer Mongolia, perhaps."

Other parents describe the teen years in different ways. "You never look good enough to be seen with your kids, groaned one mother, "but then, Sophia Loren wouldn't look good enough to be seen with them."

"A couple of years ago I was telling myself I can hardly remember when I had to comb my daughter's hair for her," another mother added, "but now I can't even remember when she last combed her own hair."

Evidently, there are all sorts of new worries coming up as our children approach the teen-age years; we might as well be aware of this. And all of those "what ifs" are pretty likely to happen . . . What if I can't go to sleep until they get in for the night? (one article I read said the reason you can't is because you know that adolescents are able to do virtually everything you can do) . . . What if I can't win arguments with them anymore? (don't try; they still don't make enough sense for fights to be worth the effort) . . . What if they rebel?

Pastoral counselor Kenneth Story tells us that rebellion is an integral part of adolescent development, the means by which a child can finally separate from his family of origin. The teen years, therefore, are the years when the child feels a need to fully check out his values against various reference centers, primarily his peer group. Sometimes, the child's rebellion takes on a mild form, like dressing in funny clothes or choosing a college far from home or hanging around with strange friends to see what Mom and Dad will do.

If a teen-ager is actually hurting himself, his family, or society during his period of rebellion, most experts agree that the child needs professional help. If he isn't, a less drastic course of action may work—like being there for the child, and expecting some conflict as part of the parenting job, and trying to put oneself in the child's shoes and, thus, avoid overreacting.

One mother sat her teen-age daughter's boy friend down and talked to him about his sexual responsibilities before the couple's first date. Needless to say, the daughter will probably be thirty-five before she speaks to her mother again.

Another parent stocked his book shelves with drug literature and talked with several counselors after having noticed a glassy-eyed look on his teenager's face. As it turned out, the boy was not on drugs at all but was, rather, in love.

It is easy to understand these parents. They are simply asking themselves questions, the same questions all of us ask. Questions like, "What if he doesn't choose a mate who will love him as much as I do? What if he decides to become a rock musician in spite of it all? What if he says no to my religion?"

"Most parents find their children's rebellion and separation processes *very* difficult to accept," explains Dr. Story, "because parenting, in a very real sense, is like sustaining one loss after another; and it is no fun to wake up one day and realize you are quickly losing control, autonomy, and power over your children."

Then, when we finally do come to terms with all this, when we have finally figured out how to prepare ourselves for the day when our children will move out of the house, even this doesn't always happen.

We are now firmly ensconced in the era of the single lifestyle, the era of postponed marriage, the era of lack of affordable housing. Many young adults, therefore, are no longer moving out of their parents' homes. Or they are moving out and then moving back, sending their parents almost nonstop from the early school years straight into the "boomerang years." Some parents contend that dealing with the new pressures involved in this kind of arrangement can be even worse than spending your life receiving collect calls from your kids.

Our children are products of us, both biologically and environmentally. They have to grow up the same way we did—making their own mistakes. Knowing this doesn't make our jobs as parents any easier, but it can prevent us from being too hard on ourselves. And who among us would turn down a little boost?

I certainly have those days when I feel like a total failure as a parent, even though I know, down deep, that my refrigerator door in itself proves that I am a good mother. It is covered with artwork only a mother could love. And I really do love that artwork, every squiggly line and every smeared "I luv you, Mommy." Other parents feel the same way. I know they do. The hard part lies in developing the inner resources that free you up to give yourself over to that love.

"When am I ever going to learn how to be a really good parent?" I mumbled to myself during one of my off days. I was so wrapped up in my mumbling that I didn't even realize Becky had walked into the room.

"What did you ask me?" Becky inquired.

"It was a rhetorical question," I said, but she didn't know what that meant, so she answered it anyway.

"I love you, Mommy," she giggled, throwing her arms around my neck. "You're the best mommy in the whole world."

I'm not the best mommy in the whole world, of course. But, at that moment, she had me convinced. In fact, I felt so secure in my parenting role that I suddenly found myself caught in motherhood's danger zone. The next part is predictable.

At odd moments during the day, those all-too-familiar little words kept popping into my head: "Maybe I have it all together as a mother after all. . . . Maybe I could even handle another baby. . . . Another soft, snuggly little bundle from heaven." The moral of the story? I had that other baby this year—a soft, snuggly little boy bundle from heaven. But he's not always soft and snuggly. Sometimes he's smelly and fussy. Just like my daughter was. Just like all babies are.

So, go ahead and ask me: "Are you sorry you found yourself in the danger zone? Are you sorry you made the decision you did?" And miss the chance to give birth to the *two* most beautiful children in the world? You've got to be kidding!

I really believe that being a parent can be both effective and fun. True, you have to keep working at it. You have to keep reminding yourself that God is in it with you—all the way. And, you have to remember that the entire world is going to be affected by the way today's parents choose to live their lives—before their children and with their children. Throughout the scuff-mark years and far beyond.

Notes

1. Veronica Thomas, "Mommy, It's Not Fair!" *Ladies' Home Journal,* February, 1985, p. 38.
2. Terri Fields, "A Mommy Is a Type of Person," *Family Circle,* May 18, 1982, p. 12.
3. Judith Viorst, "Open Mouth, Insert Foot," *Redbook,* October, 1983, p. 68.
4. David Milofsky, "What Makes a Good Family?" *Redbook,* August, 1981, pp. 58–62.
5. Dolores Curran, "What Good Families Are Doing Right," *McCall's,* March, 1983, pp. 138–140.
6. " 'Parent Burnout': Latest Signs of Today's Stresses," *U.S. News & World Report,* March 7, 1983, p. 77.
7. Bruce Feirstein, *Real Men Don't Eat Quiche* (New York: Pocket Books, 1982), pp. 15–16.
8. Larry Potts, Unpublished Baccalaureate Sermon, Cairo High School, Cairo, Illinois, 1966.
9. Claire Safran, "Why Religious Women Are Good Lovers," *Redbook,* April, 1976, pp. 103; 155–159.

For Further Reading

Benson, Dennis and Stewart, Stan. *Ministry of the Child.* Nashville, Tennessee: Abingdon, 1979.

Dobbins, Richard. *Venturing Into a Child's World.* Old Tappan, New Jersey: Flemming J. Revell, 1984.

Dobson, James. *The Strong-Willed Child.* Wheaton, Illinois: Tyndale, 1978.

Gaither, Gloria and Dobson, Shirley. *Let's Make a Memory.* Waco, Texas: Word Books, 1983.

Leman, Kevin. *Making Children Mind without Losing Yours.* Old Tappan, New Jersey: Flemming J. Revell, 1984.

Narramore, Bruce. *Help! I'm a Parent.* Grand Rapids, Michigan: Zondervan, 1972.

Stromman, Merton P. and A. Irene. *Five Cries of Parents.* San Francisco: Harper & Row, 1985.

Swindoll, Charles. *You and Your Child.* Nashville, Tennessee: Thomas Nelson, 1977.

The following trademarks were used in this book:

Aigner® Etienne
Amtrak® Amtrak Distribution Center
Band-Aid® © Johnson & Johnson Products, Inc.
Barbie® © Mattel
Big Bird® ® Sesame Street © Children's Television Network © Muppets
Big Mac® © McDonald's Corp.
Black & Decker® Black & Decker Inc.
Cabbage Patch Kids® © Original Appalachian Artworks, mfg. for Coleco
    Industries Inc.
Campbell's® Campbell Soup Co.
Care Bear™ ® Kenner © American Greetings Corp.
Cinderella © Walt Disney Productions
DIXIE® cup James River Corporation Dixie Products Group
Donald Duck © Walt Disney Productions
Ewok™ ® Star Wars © Lucas Films LTD (LFL)
Geritol® Beecham Products, Div. of Beecham Inc.
G. I. Joe® © Hasbro Industries, Inc.
Girl Scouts® Girl Scouts of the U.S.A.
He-Man® © M
JELL-O® General Foods Corp.
Keebler® © Keebler Company
Ken® © Mattel
Kentucky Fried Chicken® KFC Corporation
Kool-Aid® General Foods Corporation
McDonalds® © McDonalds Corporation
Monopoly® © Parker Brothers Division of CPG Products Corp.
Pepsi® Pepsico, Inc.
Play-Doh® CPG Products Corporation. A subsidiary of General Mills Inc. by
    its Division Kenner Products
Pudding Pops® Jell-O® General Foods Corporation
Purple Pieman® Strawberry Shortcake™ Names are trademarks of American
    Greetings Corp.
Radio Shack® A Division of Tandy Corp.
Raggedy Ann® © Bobbs-Merrill
Scrabble® Sentence Game for Juniors® © Selchow & Righter Co.
Shirt Tales® © Hallmark Cards
Smurf™ © Peyo Wallace Berrie and Co. Inc.
Snickers® Dist. by M&M Mars Div. of Mars, Inc.
Snoopy® © United Features Syndicate, Inc.
Sprite® A Product of the Coca-Cola Company
Star Wars® © Lucas Films LTD (LFL) Div. of CPG Products
Strawberry Shortcake™ ® Kenner © American Greetings Corp.
Tonka® © Tonka Corporation
Tootsie Roll Pops® Tootsie Roll Industries, Inc.
Trivial Pursuit® © Horn Abbot Ltd.

185